No Fear
In My
Classroom

No Fear
In My
Classroom

A Teacher's Guide on How to:
- Ease Students' Concerns
- Handle Parental Problems
- Focus on Education
- Gain Confidence in Yourself

Frederick C. Wootan
author of *Not In My Classroom*

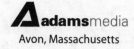
Avon, Massachusetts

To Jim Kodros, counselor, coach, teacher, but most of all friend.

Published by
Adams Media, a division of F+W Media, Inc.
57 Littlefield Street, Avon, MA 02322. U.S.A.
www.adamsmedia.com

ISBN 10: 1-59869-882-6
ISBN 13: 978-1-59869-882-4

Printed in the United States of America.

J I H G F E D C B A

Library of Congress Cataloging-in-Publication Data
is available from the publisher.

This publication is designed to provide accurate and authoritative information
with regard to the subject matter covered. It is sold with the understanding that
the publisher is not engaged in rendering legal, accounting, or other professional advice. If legal advice or other expert assistance is required, the services
of a competent professional person should be sought.
        —From a *Declaration of Principles* jointly adopted by a Committee of the
American Bar Association and a Committee of Publishers and Associations

Many of the designations used by manufacturers and sellers to distinguish their
product are claimed as trademarks. Where those designations appear in this
book and Adams Media was aware of a trademark claim, the designations have
been printed with initial capital letters.

Appendix A contains material adapted and abridged from *The Everything® New
Teacher Book*, by Melissa Kelly, copyright © 2004 by F+W Media, Inc., ISBN
10: 1-59337-033-4, ISBN 13: 978-1-59337-033-6.

This book is available at quantity discounts for bulk purchases.
For information, please call 1-800-289-0963.

Acknowledgments

It is only since entering the teaching field that I have come to realize the value in having all those years working in America's corporate sector. Experience in the world of commerce as well as the private world of family has been a great teacher. I truly believe we learn best from what we do wrong. Our successes are quickly forgotten, but our mistakes never leave us. The world teaches us, sometimes gently and sometimes harshly, and we grow from it. I thank everyone with whom I've had the honor of associating.

I especially want to thank my Principal Mrs. Catherine Mulligan for her willingness to let me use my talents in teaching the wide variety of subjects of High School English for freshmen and junior students, Public Speaking, Yearbook Class, Publications Class, General Business, Study Skills, Creative Writing, and Literature on Film, Contemporary American Issues, and Writers Workshop.

I also want to thank my editor, Brendan O'Neill for his continued encouragement and use of his expert editorial skills to make this the best presentation possible.

***

Your task as teacher is daunting, to say the least. Your students bring all kinds of fears they don't understand into your classroom. Their parents suffer from fears of a modern world filled with terror and not knowing what it will do to their children. Our great country offers fantastic opportunities, but does so within a paradigm where evil thrives.

I wrote this book to heighten awareness of fears influencing your ability to teach with the hope that knowledge of them will bring understanding and will lessen your fears thereby enhancing the learning environment of your classroom. I acknowledge that most of you deal with these daily. I applaud your efforts.

Contents

The Source of Your Fears

While researching for this book I ran across an interesting comment made more than 2,300 years ago by Aristotle. He stated:

> Confusing questions arise out of the education that actually prevails, and it is not at all clear whether the pupils should practice pursuits that are practically useful, or morally edifying, or higher accomplishments— for all these views have the support of some judges.

I guess wondering about or questioning the field of education didn't begin with me.

Franklin Delano Roosevelt said in his 1933 Inaugural Address, "The only thing we have to fear is fear itself." He knew that we needed to take drastic measures to save a flagging economy and society and that society had to set aside its fears and move boldly ahead. He worked to learn about the country's fears and experimented with ways to deal with them. As a teacher, you must continue working and searching to ferret out fears so that you will become a better educator in a society evolving more rapidly than ever before.

Do you as a teacher have fears? Of course you do. Many of you question overall government encroachment into the educational process. Many of you wonder if budget cuts will remove you from the classroom or make obtaining the equipment you need even harder. Many of you fear not getting your message across to your students so they can learn and progress in their knowledge. These and many more of your fears intertwine with those of your students, their parents, and society.

A Student's Fears

Some children cannot focus on being students in your classrooms because they fear leaving their homes due to street violence in their neighborhoods. Others fear their home environments and actually prefer to be at school, no matter how difficult. Many fear the school bullies, the peer pressures, the scholastic pressure on their time, the lack of friends, and on and on. It's important to recognize and understand the implications of these and many more potential student fears in order to educate the students.

You've probably realized that your students are no longer just preoccupied with learning in your classroom. Instead, they have become so riddled with fear they can't learn. It may be that they are so consumed by grades because their only focus is getting into college and making the "big bucks." They may have parents who inadvertently (or otherwise) warped their value systems by giving them everything they wanted, and now their only focus is on material things. These and a myriad of other worries have made them not really care about gaining knowledge for the sake of learning.

Children cannot express such a complex feeling as fear very well. It's important to know the signs and that these will depend on the age and sex of the child and so will vary as the child matures. Some examples are:

- A child just entering elementary school may cling tightly to his mom before finally letting go to enter your classroom. This child may have a fear of separation because of a recent death in his family. Abstract concepts like death are normally difficult for any adolescent to understand.

- Another child may draw pictures of his family with someone missing, or a person's head either missing or with more than one head. This usually signals that someone important to this child has recently left him.

- An older adolescent, in fifth to eighth grade, who is suffering from some form of child abuse, may gradually become anxious about taking tests or speaking in class when called upon and even become physically ill while in school.

- A normally social student may begin to withdraw because of fear of a bully, actually becoming a loner type whose grades begin to plummet.

A Parent's Fears

I have said to my wife many times that I am happy that our children are raised, but that now I worry about their children, our grandchildren. My children, now adults, must have a constant concern for the safety of their own children. Their safety is not only in jeopardy while on a school bus, which may be driven by a dope addict or convicted felon; their fellow classmates may have psychological problems that could cause psychotic behavior, or there could even be a child predator lurking near the schoolyard, trying to lure unsuspecting children into his or her car.

Some of the parents' or guardians' fears will never become known unless something upsetting happens to their child. You don't want to wait for that event to happen without knowing the potential for it.

On top of all those sometimes imaginative but justifiable and very real fears, parents must also worry about the level of education provided to their children. They need to be certain that their children have access to all the opportunities this country has to offer, and that starts with a good education.

Society-Fueled Fear

Will you have the necessary backing of the kind of education system needed to provide our great country with individuals capable of handling the problems of the future and to compete effectively in a global economy? Will those children in your classrooms know how to deal with the rising hatred for our way of life as they reach adulthood? So many more people in this world belong to the "have-nots" than the "haves"; can we consider it absurd that their feelings of frustration have developed into hatred? If we don't provide the education to understand the many elements that foster hatred for our way of life, our future as a free society becomes problematic.

You must have an awareness of government-mandated educational requirements whether or not you agree with them. Even though your goals should equal those of the parents and the government, it won't always appear that they do. You need to know how each element of society has come to its position and understanding. Unfortunately, much of the time, those goals resulted from fear.

Your Fear

How on earth do you deal with all these fears? Responding to this question is the subject matter of this book. I assure you no one person has all the answers, but the fact that you are reading this book tells me you understand the complexities of fear and want to do the best you can to educate, motivate, and maybe even inspire your students and your own children.

Many of you may have fears that thus far have surfaced only as feelings of anxiety. You feel anxious about what you teach, how you teach, and how the administration perceives the way you do these things. However, these fears manifest and build until, ultimately, they negatively affect your performance as a teacher. The goal is to rid yourself of these fears before they take a toll on your teaching.

THE FEAR How on earth do I wrap my head around all this fear?

THE SOLUTION Knowledge of the sources of fear will equip you to better deal with it. Breaking down the basic elements of the sources into mind-manageable chunks will make it possible.

LET'S SUMMARIZE . . .

❶ The problems creating fear in your classroom are not new.

❷ The problems vary widely across this country.

❸ Knowledge of these fears is the best way to deal with them.

PART I

Personal Fears

You have these before your students

even walk through the door

———————

———————

———————

CHAPTER 1

Is My Classroom an Effective Learning Environment?

Thomas Jefferson sat down to write the Declaration of Independence after long and arduous discussions with his colleagues Benjamin Franklin, John Adams, and other Founding Fathers. They all brought different viewpoints and opinions to those discussions, but they all agreed they wanted to establish a country that provided equal opportunity for all; a country run by its people, not a people run by a government. This meant abject defiance of England's King George, and then the construction of a classless and educated society.

Like our Founding Fathers, everyone has a slightly different view of what "classless society" means today. Some focus only on the idea that it means everyone is created equal, with the same basic human rights. Some take it one step further and believe achieving a classless society requires overall equality ensured by a central government that provides these human rights to all. And then there are those who say the classless theory applies to the overall welfare of a nation with a diverse people working in varying levels, but with the potential to achieve whatever level they desire, limited only by their personal talents and how well they choose to use them. However, whatever theory they espouse, they all agree that in order for this country to remain a democracy, it must have an educated populace.

Is it such a stretch then to think that classrooms *could* have different learning environments created by the dynamic of the individual teacher and his students, but maintain the common goal of an educated populace? Shouldn't we in fact come to expect these differences, which are based on different ethnicities, regional prejudices, nations of origin, religious beliefs, races, and levels of income? Yes to both. Nevertheless, it's still logical that you, as the teacher in these equations, should fear making mistakes in your classroom, thereby impacting the learning environment. Let's take a look.

The Overall Picture

During the era following the American Civil War, our country's educational experience evolved from Josiah Holbrook's lyceum movement of the early nineteenth century to establishment of permanent venues for speaking to the people. At their peak after the war, the lyceums actually took on more of an entertainment purpose than educational, with shows provided by traveling entertainers such as minstrels and vaudeville acts. The public forum they created also attracted influential speakers including Susan B. Anthony and Mark Twain.

Eventually this grew into a system of public and private schools with specific rules about who must attend, when they must attend, and what they should learn. One of the amazing things about this country is its diversity, and yet our education system actually attempts to create a uniform playing field. That playing field seems unattainable even in this, a classless society. Jonathan Kozol, in his book *Savage Inequalities*, tells about many differences that exist today; differences caused by rich versus poor, by minorities versus majorities, by tax structures that support our public schools, and by teachers' skills and attitudes.

In order to defeat this fear you have about creating a better, more effective learning environment, you need to understand that the power lies in you. The playing field may be laid out before you, but it is your game.

You: The Influencer

I get up every morning and think of the two things I remember from a speech given by the great motivational speaker Zig Ziglar: "We are what goes into our minds" and "I feel fantastic, but I'm getting better." Beginning your day with feeling fantastic and also planning to feel even better during that day will penetrate your very being until it emanates from your every pore into your personal space and on into the world around you. Think of the pebble thrown into the pond. The splash is negligible, but the ripples continue outward. Become that pebble and let your enthusiasm ripple through your classroom.

If need be, write out Zig Ziglar's thoughts on a small card. Place it by your bed or next to your coffeepot. Read it every morning until your mind has absorbed it and it becomes an important part of your personality.

Recently, one of my colleagues (whom I always find in the teacher's lounge when I arrive every morning, and I get there pretty early) said something to me that made my heart grin. He is a true academic and a voracious reader who has introduced me to many very interesting books, resulting in our having some great philosophical discussions. On this particular day he responded to my cheery "Good morning!" with, "Good morning my friend. You always get my day off to a great start. I have never in my seventy years on this earth found another person who, with such few words, so early in the day, every day, could so positively influence my mood for the entire day. My students and I appreciate it."

I nearly fell over. I actually thought that some days my early morning cheeriness irritated him.

Remember the Ripple

I know I am blessed to work in a private school where most students have a stable home life, and come ready to learn. But I also know it is an artificial environment isolated from the real world. Our students generally come from households where the fear of going hungry or becoming homeless has never been an issue. Some would call them snobs. Some would call them spoiled rich kids. Some would simply have so much envy in their eyes they forget these are just kids. I will not deny that most of my students live privileged lives.

However, with privilege comes fear. These types of students have a fear of not living up to certain standards. You need to make them realize that these standards of perfection are only perceived in their young minds.

Alternatively, there are those schools with students who do live with daily hunger and sometimes even no home to go to. How do you motivate them? You may have more than thirty of these kids in your classroom. They are sleepy from not having a comfortable bed; they are angry because of the fight that took place in their home the night before. They can't concentrate because of the rumblings of their empty stomachs. Your classroom is cold because the windows won't close tight and have several cracks or broken-out panes. The aged coat of paint on the walls has faded into oblivion or is peeling off. Ceiling tiles have fallen from a leaky roof that should have been replaced or at least repaired twenty years ago.

Your students are dealing with a different type of fear. They want to survive. You need to be their rock and let out ripples of hope to assuage their fears, and in turn your fears of their not learning.

Take for Example . . .

Obviously, these very different scenarios require very different methods. Last year I became so concerned about the classroom environment my privileged students were creating that I conducted an experiment.

It was in the dead of winter and the outside temperature was in the below-freezing range. I shut my classroom door and opened the windows. I reorganized the desks, normally in a spread-out V pattern, into tight rows of nine. I placed the rows about a foot apart, and each desk touched the back of the one in front. I made cardboard signs that read "ceiling tile" and took long strings and tied them to the ceiling's support beams so they hung either in the rows between the desks or came within about a foot of where a student would sit.

I greeted the students as they came in, telling them to leave their books and whatever else they were carrying on the floor near the door and to take a seat without moving the desks or climbing on them. That meant they had to cooperate with each other and enter the room in single file.

Once they were seated I passed out five pieces of copy paper and six pencils, some with no eraser and in need of sharpening. I told them there was a wall separating them from the open space left in the room between the last row of desks and the actual wall, and they could not cross it. (I placed a strip of masking tape on the floor to represent the wall.) I also told them not to close the windows even though the room was getting cold.

Since I taught American Literature, I took out my book and began reading a poem. I read one stanza and looked up. They sat there looking at me with a mixture of disgust and puzzlement in their eyes. One asked what was going on. I answered using my sternest teacher voice, saying, "Keep quiet! I am reading, and you should be taking notes, not asking stupid questions. I intend to read this poem and then you will write an explanation for me without a copy of the book to reference." When he complained that he not only didn't have anything to write on but he didn't have anything to write with, I told him he should have brought those things with him. Of course, he responded that I had made him leave them at the door. I then began the real lesson.

I told them that for at least that class period and more, if necessary, my classroom was part of the poverty-stricken public school system of one of the poorest cities in this country. I told them about one of the finest young men I ever knew. This young man, whom I met while in the Army, was from East St. Louis, one of the poorest communities in the United States. He had plans to go to college when his tour was over and then to return to the family business of running a junkyard. He was a well-spoken, articulate man, and I had every confidence that he would achieve that objective.

As I expected, one student asked why on earth he would want to go back to such a place and, of all things, run a junkyard. I told them that, because of growing up under those circumstances, he did not know a better thing existed. He was proud of the fact that his family had a successful business. One of the kids said in a low voice to the person next to him, "What an idiot."

That was not the voice of a snob. It was the voice of a student who needed to further his education and to expand his world. At the end of class, several students asked if I was going to continue with the room that way. I then told all of them to write a paper for me telling me why they prefer the original classroom and why the friend from my past was not an idiot.

The response was great. Most of my students actually thought about what had happened that day and wrote papers reflecting those considerations. Will that brief exposure to another world make them better people? Only time will tell.

The message here is that the learning atmosphere of your classroom is up to you. If you know that your students need a soft place to land because they don't have one at home, your classroom can be that place. If your students don't need that soft place, you don't have to provide it. Remember, your obligation to them is to help make them educated citizens, and that will work best if you have them in an environment that promotes learning. In order to make sure your classroom is an effective learning environment, examine your physical site in light of what you know about your students and their outside lives, and adjust accordingly.

THE FEAR What if my students don't feel comfortable in my classroom? I'm afraid that my classroom may not be the right environment for learning. How do I reduce my students' fears and enhance the learning that takes place in my classroom?

THE SOLUTION Find out what movies and what music your students like. Find pictures that convey your interpretation of those movies and/or music. For example, I have made a collage of pictures of some of my students' favorite musicians and bands and placed it on the wall they see when they enter my classroom. When

I am giving a test or having my students work on an assignment, I play soft "easy listening" music. I switch the music to something they like that has a fast, upbeat tempo when I want them to take a break. They know I am paying attention to their world with the pictures and their music. They also learn that there are simple ways to express artistic talent such as with the collage, and to actually enjoy the peaceful calm of my "easy listening" music. Thus, I have enhanced my classroom learning environment.

LET'S SUMMARIZE . . .

❶ You have an ever-changing world that affects your classroom.

❷ You need to understand the students' world in order to provide the type of environment in your classroom that will work best.

❸ There really is no such thing as the United States school system. There are many schools of thought within an overall idea of education.

❹ You must create a learning environment in your classroom that complements both your personality and those of your students.

CHAPTER 2

Am I Bringing My Personal Life into My Professional Life?

No one expects you to have a perfect home life, where everything always goes your way. You know this, but if you fail to understand that pain is a part of life, it will penetrate into your heart and destroy your enthusiasm for whatever you do. This can result in confusion and dissatisfaction. An automatic assumption that being negative is realistic, and being positive is not, adds to your fears. Once you begin to feel this way, it destroys any sense of optimism, thereby potentially destroying your ability to provide the greatest teaching lesson possible: being the positive role model all your students need.

If you truly fear bringing what you consider to be your dysfunctional home life into your classroom, you need professional help. Seek guidance on how to fix the outside issues so they do not negatively affect your students' learning.

However, if you, like any responsible teacher, simply fear that a personal issue (such as a minor spat with your spouse or teenager, or having just discovered a loved one has a serious, life-threatening disease) may be a negative influence on your students, read on.

"Remember that much of the trick of moving from pain to power is taking action." —Susan Jeffers, *Feel the Fear—and Do It Anyway*

Frank Leahy, one of the most successful football coaches in the history of the University of Notre Dame, said, "When the going gets tough, let the tough get going." So, just how tough do you have to be? You need to be tough enough to find ways to distance yourself from those personal problems so that they do not come down on your students.

After many years of racking my unknowing male brain trying to immediately solve any problem that my wife talked about, I finally got the message. Women don't always expect guys to solve every problem they talk about. They like to talk about their problems, but, as I now know, they may not be looking for a solution. They may just be venting. (Or what guys call "thinking out loud.")

While venting is important in your personal relationships, *do not vent to or around your students*. This "no venting" rule applies to all teachers of students of any age. The last thing you want is for a student's concern that you have a dying sister to distract his concentration from your lecture or classroom exercise. This may seem harsh, but it is what it is.

When It Is Acceptable

Now, if you are going to have a surgical procedure or some illness that will prevent you from coming to school for an extended period of time, you should tell your students that you expect to be out for a while. If they are under the age of thirteen, you will want to reassure them that you will be back, and that you will send them an update from time to time.

Informing your students about a personal issue that will affect the classroom is acceptable. You just need to handle this communication in a professional manner.

Take for Example . . .

Recently I discovered that I had some sort of problem with my legs. Having been a long-distance runner and in very good health all my life, I am certain that the day I hobbled into school leaning very heavily on a cane, my students were concerned. At first, all I knew was that I had been experiencing severe pains shooting down my legs and on that morning, when I attempted to get out of bed, I nearly hit the floor. My legs just seemed not to be there. I struggled to regain my balance and bought a cane on my way to school.

My wife made a doctor's appointment for later that day after begging me to stay home, but I stubbornly refused. I explained the cane by telling the kids that I had fallen while running that morning and thought I had a sprained ankle. After numerous tests over the next month and some wonder drug that actually allowed me to walk, albeit very slowly and with my trusty cane, I learned that my many years of long-distance running had destroyed the disks in the lumbar region of my spine. That was the bad news. The good news was that a surgical procedure could fix it.

Once I had the news and the date of surgery I told my students what was happening to me and that I would be out for at least six weeks. I teach juniors and seniors in high school and I felt comfortable sharing that with them. I also told them I would arrange all their classes and dictate my lectures, coordinated with the outlines I would have on the Smart Board. I heard a sigh, and I like to think it was a sigh of relief, not because they didn't want the opportunity to have the reduced amount of work that typically comes with a substitute, but because they knew what to expect. (Oh, and the surgery worked.)

Dealing with Divorce

I have not experienced this life-altering event and thank God daily for that, but I realize I am actually in the minority. The average child today will experience a breakup of the family unit at least once by the age of eighteen. The fact that you could go through a divorce would come as no surprise to them, but if it does happen, the less they know about it the better.

It must be extremely difficult to contain the overwhelming emotions connected with divorce. During my years in corporate America I often worked either with or for someone going through a divorce, and found that the person in this situation could not concentrate much of the time. He lost his focus, the employer lost the employee's productivity, and if the employee were in management, the employer also lost the productivity of the sufferer's subordinates. Your classroom, however, is not corporate America. You are the manager and your students are the employees. You don't want to add your students' productivity to the list of casualties caused by your divorce.

If you are struggling with a divorce, it will inevitably happen that a student will come to you and ask for an exception to completing a homework assignment because he or she went to mom or dad's home last night and left the book at the other parent's house. If you have a rule about homework being in on time, do you make an exception? Your heart will definitely want to make the exception without further thought. Your mind will tell you that making this exception excuses the child of divorce, while not doing so will teach the child responsibility in the face of adversity.

Who wins out? Remember, you made the rules, so you can break them. If you feel that the student is telling the truth, give her the exception. However, make this judgment call as a teacher, not as a divorced person.

THE FEAR I am going through a messy divorce. My husband wants shared custody of our children; he won't speak to me; he's stopped making our house payments since I made him move out. I feel completely exhausted when I get up in the morning, and stay that way all day. I know I'm not giving my students their full measure of teaching, but I just can't help it.

THE SOLUTION First of all, seek help from an outside professional to handle the disputes that are arising out of your divorce.

In terms of your classroom, you obviously can't hide this from your students. No matter how young they are, they can tell that you are in pain. They may very likely feel responsible for it. So, you need to take decisive action to regain your ability to handle yourself properly in your classroom. Discuss a leave of absence with your principal so you can straighten out your outside life without jeopardizing your students in the process.

LET'S SUMMARIZE . . .

❶ Everyone experiences pain, either physical or mental, at some time in life. Don't ignore it.

❷ While you never want to vent your problems to your students, there may be circumstances involving your health when you need to tell them.

❸ If you find yourself going through a divorce, don't share the problems related to it with your students. Most of them either are experiencing or have experienced a breakup of the family unit, and you may be the one person who represents stability in their lives.

CHAPTER 3

Can I Count on Job Security?

The following headline should disturb you: "Dayton Board Lays Off 208 Teachers." The article discusses what happened as a result of the recent defeat of the school district's operating levy. Beyond the teacher layoffs, 87 aides, 29 people in administrative jobs, 18 in non-teaching, non-administrative positions, and 51 adjunct teaching staff were let go; in addition, another 35 teachers resigned or retired and would not be replaced. How are you supposed to concentrate on educating our future Americans when there is such an alarming rate of education layoffs across the country?

You can't look to the government for support. In fact, there's an inadvertent negative effect of government funding for poor, predominantly minority students who were functioning below grade level, such as those who qualify for Title IV of the Civil Rights Act of 1964. If you do what you should do as a teacher, and succeed in elevating those students' performance to grade level, the school district may have its Title IV budget cut, leaving no financial support for the program. Title IV, and comparable programs that tie money to student failure, don't have a way to deal with student success except to terminate the funding. That means no funding for other students who still need the help. It may also mean the loss of a teaching position.

In order for the schools to qualify for funding for students with learning disabilities, they must have documented evidence that such a need exists. A student who may just need additional support but is not learning disabled is nevertheless labeled as such for documentation purposes. We have created a system that makes it "educationally beneficial" to label children as learning disabled. This labeling has a negative impact on the students; however, it is important in order to receive government funding. As a teacher looking out for your students and your job, you are caught in the middle of a Catch-22.

How Did We Get Here?

We all know how important education is to a democratic society. Making informed decisions about our daily lives and, more important, about the election of our representatives to government is essential to a successful democracy. Although our public school system seems riddled with problems, it has served this country well. When Horace Mann used his seemingly boundless energy to improve public schools back in the nineteenth century, he didn't do so expecting the schools to fail. He, like Thomas Jefferson, realized the value of an educated populace.

Mann, as a state senate president, had to deal with poorly equipped schoolhouses and untrained teachers. He worked for the Massachusetts Board of Education to equalize educational opportunities by putting in place more training for teachers, lengthening the school year, and finding ways to fund increased teacher salaries, better books, and school repairs. He was passionate about the concept of learning.

The public school system started on the local level. At first, only the wealthy took advantage of it; it seemed only the wealthy realized the value of education. It wasn't until nearly the end of the nineteenth century that free public elementary education became compulsory. Private education systems began to flourish only after the 1925 Supreme Court ruling in *Pierce v. Society of Sisters*, which established that mandatory attendance at school included private as well as public schools. At about the same time, the demand for skilled workers caused attendance to rise at American high schools as well as elementary.

The need for higher levels of education grew rapidly during the twentieth century, giving rise to government financial support for state universities. The G.I. Bill, enacted after World War II to assist war veterans in obtaining a college education, added to the country's interest in post–high school education. This was followed by the National Defense Education Act of 1958 and the aforementioned Civil Rights Act of 1964, both of which improved the financing of public schools.

Have all these well-intentioned actions gone astray? Or, have advancements in technology and learning methods not kept up with societal issues, causing an upheaval in the teaching profession and education systems?

One thing is for certain. No one can take away an education. Another certainty is that our country is growing. We have an expanding population and economy that demands an educated work force. So, if you lose your job at the end of a school year, there is more than likely another position in education that needs to be filled.

Who Needs Us?

According to the United States Bureau of Labor Statistics there is an expected increase of the U.S. civilian non-institutional population by 23.9 million over the 2004–2014 periods, a slower rate of growth than during both the 1994–2004 and 1984–1994 periods.

There will be population growth, which means more students, resulting in a need for more teachers. According to the U.S. Bureau of Labor Statistics, the education and health services sector is projected to grow faster than any other sector, increasing 30.6 percent between 2004 and 2014.

This is hardly a perfect picture, though. Our society is weighed down by inequalities due to unjustified prejudices, discrimination, crime, violence, and a decaying infrastructure. Even our education system is not safe. We have managed to corrupt or distort the laws passed by every well-intentioned leader, and there is no reason to believe this will cease as long as human nature exists.

The most recent federal legislation to have a wide effect on education is No Child Left Behind, and it continues to be a point of controversy. Margaret Spellings, the United States Secretary of Education, has said that nearly 500,000 more students have learned basic math skills and another 500,000 get free tutoring, and parents of some 50 million students have more information, more control, and more choices about their children's education than before the act became law.

On the other hand, according to an Associated Press report on FOX News, more than a fourth of our schools failed to meet the requirements of adequate improvement. This statistic is interesting because the states have the flexibility to design the test, and can make their state's test easier than those of other states, allowing for a better likelihood that they will meet the federal requirements. How can we as a nation know if the law really works if the basis for measuring its success varies from state to state?

We can't. It's this inability that adds to your incalculable fears, resulting in your insecurity.

Insecurity Comes from Without; Security Comes from Within

The one most important factor overlooked by this history and social studies lesson is the skill it takes to create a learning environment and to be personally secure in your career path. That comes from your heart as well as your head. Mike Krzyzewski says in his book *Leading with the Heart*:

> *If you're always striving to achieve a success that is defined by someone else, I think you'll always be frustrated . . . . The only way to get around such an unhappy ending is to continually define your own success.*

Once you firmly implant that message, you will gain the self-confidence needed to remain a successful teacher for a lifetime. Does that mean you continue to do things exactly the way you now do them? Certainly not. Any professional in any field must continue learning and experimenting with his or her knowledge base. Embrace new information, techniques, and ideas developed by others, test them, and ask for evaluation by peers and administrators to obtain their insights. It is doing these things that will reduce or even eliminate any fear of losing your job.

A wise man once said that we all are teachers, whether we are mothers, fathers, supervisors, or corporate titans. You, however, have the specific training to teach and, as such, society places you in direct charge of its future. Our political leaders, our engineers, our surgeons, our lawyers, our scientists, and all the rest wouldn't be able to do what they do without someone having taught the subject they needed. Everyone needs a teacher. That is your job security.

Set aside all the frustrations caused by unhappy administrators, parents, and, yes, even students. Take time to remember the one thank-you from a former student, or the former student you read about who made a scientific discovery that will make mankind's life better, or a comment by a parent that his child felt you were the best teacher she had. Those are your medals; those are your bonuses. Read your newspaper and feel a warm rush when you finish an interesting article and see a former student's name in the byline. Look for the best in everyone you teach every day. You won't be disappointed.

THE FEAR What do I do if some event outside my control such as voter defeat of a school bond operating levy results in the cancellation of my teaching contract?

THE SOLUTION Remind yourself of your skills by reviewing your resume and updating it to include those skills you have added. Contact school administrators, send out your new resumes, ask for interviews, and sell yourself. If you can't be your biggest promoter, your skills could go without proper notice. Remind yourself that the heart surgeon couldn't have learned his unique skills without many teachers along the way.

LET'S SUMMARIZE . . .

❶ There will be news that will shake your confidence.

❷ Our Founding Fathers knew that for a free nation to succeed it must have an educated populace.

❸ Our form of government has fostered different viewpoints. That leads to controversy and can lead to uncertainty and anxiety about keeping your job due to public policy affecting school funding.

❹ Your security lies within your heart, and your focus on the learning of your students.

❺ It is that focus that will allow you to concentrate on your task, thereby reducing or eliminating your feeling of job insecurity.

CHAPTER 4

How Do I Handle a Difficult Administrator?

Do not create an epic battle with your boss. There is an old expression in the business world (which I've cleaned up here): Don't urinate into the wind. True, it's a cliché, but most well-worn expressions hold some truth, so it certainly warrants serious consideration. However, nothing is always black or white. Here's a personal example of an exception to the old adage.

Not too many years ago I accepted an executive position with a medium-size corporation. My job involved marketing management of a very large geographic territory. I reported to the director of national marketing, who in turn reported directly to the president and CEO of the company. As it turns out, I had personal and professional ethical differences with the director. These differences forced me to make a decision: Quit or fight. I felt the future of the company depended on my fighting, even at the risk of losing my job.

I conducted my fight by ensuring that every decision I made was above reproach both professionally and ethically, and I made sure the CEO was aware of that fact. I also conducted myself ethically (as I always have, so this wasn't difficult) and made sure that other employees observed my actions. Although it didn't happen overnight, the entire culture of the company changed due to my standing up against the management.

Lower-level employees take their lead from those in charge. They naturally want to emulate their superiors, and the carpet leading to my office door became well worn. This wonderful result not only improved the reputation of the company and the overall morale of the employees, but the director resigned. I consider this one of my greatest accomplishments.

Not everyone wants to be a crusader, but we all can focus our attention on our professional goals, either with the approval of our superiors or without it. Keep in mind that a struggle of wills definitely detracts from the learning going on in the classroom.

Egocentric Motives Rule

Keeping in mind that everyone has an agenda will benefit you and your fellow teachers in collectively moving forward in the quest to educate. It is a collective effort because we are social creatures living in a society constructed for us by others. You must, therefore, learn as much as you can about that society and how you fit into it.

As I am sure you already know, we live under the philosophy that everyone has the right to life, liberty, and the pursuit of happiness. Over the years, as we have evolved in our individual beliefs both morally and legally, we have continually redefined the meaning of those three tenets of freedom.

Combining the fact that every human being has a basic desire to live unencumbered by the actions of other human beings with the fact that our modern culture has produced occasionally overzealous watchdogs of our freedoms, it is no wonder we now have difficulty speaking without offending someone or some group. What does this push to political correctness have to do with you? Everything.

As an example I remember an experience with "My Old Kentucky Home," written by Stephen C. Foster, our first American songwriter, which included the word "darkies." When I addressed this classic in my English class, I led the class in singing it. However, I stumbled over the absence of the word "darkies." Somewhere along the way someone who apparently matters to the American literature scene decided to change that word to "people." Perhaps he or she did so because the song actually should have included white migrant workers, or because some African Americans might become offended. I guess I have to wonder who really has the right to take the literary license to change an original American classic. I believe we should make every attempt possible not to deliberately offend anyone while teaching, but does it extend that far? When will someone who matters change all those offending words in *The Adventures of Huckleberry Finn* to make it politically correct?

> The inclusion of offensive language as read in original texts can be a great way to open conversations about tolerance. It allows students to see how groups have been treated and how we can better our society.

It should be your desire, as it is mine, to share with your students something about your subject you are dying to tell them without fear of reprisals from an administrator. The one characteristic of great public speakers is their ability to inspire due to their passion for their subject. The question then becomes: how to do this effectively and remain employed? The answer lies in understanding the administrator's role.

The Administrator's Conundrum

It has been said that trying to please or at least not upset everyone is a fool's journey. On the other hand, in today's political environment, where it often seems the minority rules, upsetting even one person can result in untold damage. So, what is the school principal to do? The choices are more numerous than I can illustrate appropriately in this book, but here are just a few:

1. Ignore societal pressures for political correctness and go with "the gut."

2. Become intimately familiar with all the legal ramifications of political correctness in light of the obligations to fulfill the mission and goals of the state and national departments of education, requirements of the board of education, and goals of the school.

3. Become a generalist in the knowledge of the mission, laws, and societal norms, thereby pushing the responsibility for the intimate knowledge level down to the classroom teachers and holding them accountable. (Passing the buck!)

4. Use management skills learned by formal education and by implementing appropriate practices, allowing for the potential benefits to education and accepting any possible political repercussions.

5. Rigidly structure the curriculum to be followed, allowing for no deviation by teachers, and thus rely on this as the basic defense of societal claims if needed.

6. Allow parents to rule by avoiding confrontations, and hope the end result will be acceptable levels of learning without other societal pressures.

7. Take the position of enforcing district, state, and federal guidelines and regulations as the reason for inhibiting good classroom practices, or in other terms, copping out.

How do your administrator's worries affect your own? Let's examine the preceding points to see their effect on you and your educational priorities.

THE GOING WITH "THE GUT" APPROACH

The first instance has the administrator taking on an enormous risk in order to follow his instincts about what it takes to create an excellent school environment conducive to above-average learning. As long as the state testing verifies the result, he will be satisfied with these efforts. You will be sheltered from all the pressure coming from school officials, parents, and other interested parties in the community. However, when the situation arises wherein any of the many forms of perceived injustice toward the student occurs, the administrator will find himself in deep trouble.

THE LEGAL APPROACH

In the second situation the administrator will become so mired down in the minutiae of the law and its implementation that no administering will happen. You will probably wonder where he or she went, leaving you without guidance.

THE "PASSING THE BUCK" APPROACH

You will experience the third situation up close and personal when allegations of misconduct or other unprofessional practice arise. The administrator will hold off the attack with generalities until it gets ugly, and then it will be your turn.

THE ADMINISTRATOR/MANAGER APPROACH

If you have an administrator who espouses number four in the preceding list, you should never leave him or her. This administrator will be applying all the skills at his or her disposal in learning and maintaining knowledge of potential societal/legal issues while at the same time providing you with the guidelines within which you can comfortably teach. If some kind of issue does surface, this administrator will back you up and will know the appropriate corrective actions to take to deal with the problem. Don't let him or her down.

THE "MY WAY, OR THE HIGHWAY" APPROACH

If your administrator abides by number five, he or she has established structure or rules for following the curriculum and other school rules that are rigid and inflexible; woe to the violator.

THE PARENTAL RULE APPROACH

Once the administrator takes path number six, the parents will take over. You will have had your authority undermined, making it extremely difficult to function with the passion needed to establish great learning environments in your classrooms.

THE COPPING OUT APPROACH

Finally, if your administrator always supports the superior authority, he normally does so in an attempt to protect his job. Look out if you need an immediate decision.

You can see from these few alternatives that your administrators walk a tight rope. The stress and pressure on them to satisfy a number of different people, like students, teachers, parents, and city officials, can be enormous. Therefore, in order to alleviate your fear, you must anticipate their objections.

Suppose you started to incorporate sign language in your lessons, interjected some French phrases into your lecture, or moved all the desks to one side of the room so you and your students could sit together on the floor. If one of your students disagreed with your new practice and brought her objection to your administrator, it is likely that he will confront you about it with disapproval. What do you do? You need to be able to explain that this new method has an educational purpose, share with him the intended results, and show him how it builds on the classroom experience. Don't be afraid; just be prepared.

> Having well-thought-out plans puts you in the driver's seat. Being able to clearly explain how a new, unorthodox plan will help your teaching will alleviate any fears you may have about an administrator's objections.

I am not attempting to call a thorn a rose by telling you that your administrator will always agree with you. However, proper preparation will not only make you a better teacher, but will help alleviate your fear of reprisal from your administrator for having tried something new. It takes courage, but it's worth the effort.

THE FEAR It's important to assign my students science homework, so they can increase their understanding of the terminology and its application. Yet, every time a parent complains about the amount of homework assigned, my principal asks me to try to find ways to reduce the workload rather than stand by my philosophy.

THE SOLUTION It sounds like you have already expressed your philosophy to your principal and it fell on deaf ears. Now would be a good time to rethink your teaching methods. Have you utilized your class time in the best way possible? In other words, could you work any of the currently assigned homework into a period of student self-study? If there are other science teachers in your school, check with them to find out how much homework time they require of their students. Can you incorporate the work done by students individually into class projects where the students have some ability to make good use of their time and find it more enjoyable, thereby reducing potential parental objections? Check out your district and state science scores to find out how your students' scores compare. Prepare for any objections by making sure you are doing the best job possible and report your findings to your administrator. This will satisfy your fear of reprisals as well as knowing you are doing a good job. It will also better equip your administrator to deal with any complaints reducing, or maybe even eliminating, any need to discuss them with you.

LET'S SUMMARIZE . . .

❶ Make sure you pick your battles with administrators. Losing is the normal result of disagreements with them.

❷ Man by nature has an egocentric agenda, so work at understanding.

❸ Gain knowledge of your administrator's problems and methods of dealing with them.

❹ Center your teaching on the student.

CHAPTER 5

Do I Need to Know How to Use All This Technology?

WUT^? N2M W/ ME.

If reading these seemingly random letters and symbols leaves you feeling dumbfounded, don't be afraid. You may be wondering how you, an intelligent, educated person, can feel such fear from being completely befuddled by something so silly. After all, if the students in your classroom can communicate as such, shouldn't you? You're the only one who has experienced both adolescence and adulthood. Shouldn't you know all the symbols of the digital age?

The answer is simple: No, you shouldn't.

Jay Leno tells a story about being watched by a group of curious teenagers while he filled his 1913 Mercer with gasoline. The kids simply couldn't understand why he put gasoline into it, since gasoline couldn't have been invented in 1913. Remember, this thinking comes from a generation raised with laptops, cell phones, iPods, text messaging, multifunctional calculators, and video games. Just as it's understandable that they can't comprehend the fact that Leno's car runs on gas, it's understandable that you can't comprehend their text message lingo. (By the way, "WUT^? N2M W/ ME" means "What's up? Not too much with me.")

Use Technology to Your Advantage

You can't let not understanding new technology become ignorance. Using these new digital devices will help to make your classroom an effective learning environment. Hoping they will go away will not.

Reaching nearly my wits' end with a classroom of students struggling to learn, I resorted to searching the web for something that would help. At first I went to the sites recommended by our school system as ones that would support our teaching effort. Unfortunately, I found that the solutions they offered seemed to improve my teaching skills, but not my students' learning ability. Not to be deterred, I returned to the web and decided to use Google, the search engine I have come to embrace as the top of the line.

I was able to use the search engine to find interactive grammar games that my students could play. I watched them build on their skills as they played the game on the Smart Board (an interactive whiteboard that is revolutionizing classrooms). As they took turns at the board, I recorded how well each student did and, from that, I found new games that involved writing sentences and paragraphs.

During subsequent classes I brought one of the school's laptop carts into the room so each student would have a laptop to use. I instructed the students on how to access the particular games I wanted them to play, and let them all go at their own pace while I walked around making sure they stayed on task, and answering their questions.

These simple Internet games did not solve all of my students' learning issues, but they certainly helped to get them interested in the subject matter I was teaching.

Tips for Using the Web to Your Advantage

While I do not intend to teach you the ins and outs of searching the web, I do want to provide you with a helpful hint on how to entertain yet educate using the Internet. It will allow you to easily access the wealth of entertaining and educational resources that the Internet can provide. This simple tip will instill in you enough confidence about using this magnificent (yet potentially dangerous) tool that you should be relieved of any fears you may have about it.

If you have Internet access in your classroom and a monitor or Smart Board that is easily visible to all of your students, you can begin this simple Internet tutorial by going to *www.google.com*. Click in the Google search box and type in "grammar games," "math games," "science games," or whatever subject you are teaching, then click "Google Search."

The next screen will have many choices of games to play that your students will enjoy and learn from at the same time. If the resources are available, it's a simple, quick, and easy way to get unenthused students interested in the subject you are trying to teach.

Interactive Learning Systems

Obviously, there have been enormous changes made in our society that have impacted student learning. Today's students are much more kinesthetic learners than those of twenty years ago. Learning has gone through a cycle of being mostly visual to mostly audio to mostly kinesthetic; all the stages of the cycle have contained combinations of different types of learning, just with more emphasis on one than the others.

Our nation has grown from agrarian to industrial to communication-oriented to information-based and requires educational techniques that comply with the demands of these changes. The digital generation we are trying to teach has become so hands-on that they have almost constant access to information. Computerization has gone from requiring large climate-controlled, vibration-proof rooms for huge tape machines and memory banks to desktops, laptops, cell phones, WiFi, handhelds, game consoles, streaming video, Smart Boards, and smart phones.

You must be prepared to move away from your daily planner, manila folders, lined paper tablets, note pads, and all other forms of hard-copy supplies. As the digital age revolutionizes our society and our schools, there will be a push to incorporate the various new technologies into our classrooms. The only way to avoid fearing these technological advancements is by understanding how they can help make you a better teacher.

Intertwingularity

This word sums up your major fear of technology.

Intertwingularity was first coined by Ted Nelson in *Computer Lib/Dream Machines* and communicates how the interrelations in human knowledge are truly complex.

Your training as a teacher tells you to impart information that is hierarchical, categorical, or sequential, whether you or your students are right-brain or left-brain learners. It has worked for you and so it should, therefore, work for your students. Consider the very real possibility that the majority of your students, whether in elementary or high school, have become accustomed to inferential learning from a virtual world. They just don't get why you want them to do things chronologically, for example. Or why information has to be locked inside a textbook, written by someone they never heard of and published by a source they don't care about.

In his book *Discovering the Future: The Business of Paradigms*, Joel Arthur Barker states:

Two basic things happen when you step outside the boundaries. The first is that you are able to apply the prevailing paradigm rules effectively in a new, uncharted area ... in other words, you have extended the domain of the old paradigm. More problems to solve with the rules you are so good at. The second option is ... : You find that your employee has stepped into a new domain ... that will require a new paradigm to solve the problems in it.

Sure, Mr. Barker is addressing managers in his book, but the management of your classroom is really no different from the management of an office. Your students have stepped into that paradigm outside your customary teaching box, creating or increasing your fear of technology. Let them step out. If you allow them to lead to a place where they are comfortable, you will find that you can apply those forms of hierarchy and categorizing and sequencing with which you feel comfortable. This results not only in your students learning, but in you learning too.

Try enthusiastically to intertwine standard education practices with their digital world. Your enthusiasm will become infectious as the students recognize your willingness to understand their world. New knowledge expands this digital world and can enhance and even become a part of the content within your curricula if you make use of the new kinds of hardware and techniques that make your students enthusiastic about learning.

For example, when teaching my general business class about the importance of using GPS devices to keep track of the location of outside employees in industries such as trucking, service contracting, or outside sales, I asked them if any of their cell phones had this locating device. When they realized this was a common technology that could be put to good use in their current situation, they immediately understood its added value, and even began suggesting other areas outside their industries where this technology could be used.

Relate to your students that the technology that surrounds them and that they use every day can help advance their education in an entertaining way.

Some Sources to Consider

Develop your understanding of how technology can aid in your students' education by visiting these Internet resources. Keep in mind that these sites are not the only ones available, so it's in your best interest to explore additional ways you can use the world wide web to your advantage in the classroom.

A good place to start learning about interactive mobile computing is *www.goknow.com/sketchycontest*. Here you will see how you can discard the paper-and-pencil approach that has become so boring to young learners.

A wonderful site for science teachers is *http://teemss.concord.org*. Go there and try the sample activity. You and your students could do something like this by creating a podcast. Creating podcasts is a magnificent tool that allows kids to share what they've learned with each other and with a global audience. The feeling of accomplishment they get from this exercise will help them to remember this lesson forever.

The University of Massachusetts–Dartmouth has a great site for math teachers. Check it out at *www.kaputcenter.umassd .edu/products*. Their research involves math levels from pre-algebra to calculus.

Have you ever taken your class to a museum? If so, you prepared them before the trip by studying the textbook information on all the things you knew they would see in the museum. However, much of that information was lost by the time they actually were in the museum. Mobile computers that students can carry around the museum can help in this area. The downside is that if the students get too caught up in using their handheld computers, the cultural experience is lost. However, these difficulties aside, take a look at this site: *www.myartspace.org.uk.*

Some additional commercial sites that might help bridge the gap between education and technology are leapfrog.com, education.ti.com, and funbrain.com.

There are many more sites like these, but I don't want to overwhelm you; the intent is to relieve your fear of technology by demonstrating that it is here to help you.

Before ending this discussion of ways to incorporate technology into student learning, consider this thought: you can look into making yourself and your school more efficient by automating classroom attendance methods and the way in which you score homework, quizzes, and essays. This would make the information available almost immediately to students and administrators, and would allow for reports to be instantly generated.

The more you understand the advantages of incorporating technology into your classroom, the more comfortable you will be with teaching in this digital learning age.

THE FEAR I am afraid that allowing my students to use computers for assignments will take away from some of the basic knowledge they need, such as good penmanship and spelling.

THE SOLUTION You can establish the assignment in such a way that they only use the computer for notes and then must actually write the report by hand. This will give them practice in using computers, but also reinforce the need for clear penmanship and the ability to spell without a spell checker. (Research done so far actually indicates that using computers has had no negative effect on handwriting.)

LET'S SUMMARIZE . . .

❶ You have placed your nervous fingers on the keyboard and mouse and already begun to reduce the shaking.

❷ You know that the world of learning involves new ideas, and these hands-on learners love going to the Internet any way they can.

❸ A new word, *intertwingularity*, has become a part of your vernacular, and you can say it without stuttering because you understand it in concept.

❹ You have experimented with some Internet educational sources and found them very helpful, if not pedagogical.

CHAPTER 6

Am I Being Fair?

Have you ever had a student say to you that something you just told her to do wasn't fair, or your test was too hard? If you haven't, please give every teacher you know, and me, a lesson in how you do it.

It really doesn't matter how fair you make and grade your assignments; at least one student will disagree. Believe it or not, students put a lot of pressure on themselves, and have a lot of pressure being put on them by parents and peers as they go through the process of figuring out who they are. So anything can threaten them, especially a failed test. To relieve this threat (or perhaps sometimes the guilt of not studying), they try to shift the blame. Teacher unfairness becomes their defense for failure. And you know that a story of the unfairness of your assignments and grading will go directly to their parents.

To Test or Not to Test, That Is the Question

If everyone got an A on a test, did it really evaluate the knowledge gained from your teaching?

If half the class received an A on a test, could they have demonstrated more knowledge if you had given them a better test?

If everyone failed a test, do you need to re-evaluate your teaching methods, or do you just have a classroom full of kids who have no desire to learn?

Unfortunately, there's no real "right" answer to any of these questions. I have heard some teachers say that they are happy if the grades on their tests fall into the classic bell curve. Others would prefer students not to get 100 percent of the answers correct because that would mean they could've demonstrated more knowledge, but the test gave them no way to show it. So what do you do?

You give a test that measures learning. Now, how hard was that?

Relax and take a deep breath. It'll make sense. Read on.

Build Your Testing Confidence and Save Time

The teaching business has standardized methods of testing that will help reduce your very legitimate concerns for creating tests that accomplish proper assessment of student learning and, at the same time, reduce or eliminate any perceptions of unfairness. By using the help provided in preparing your rubrics, only the unprepared student will proclaim unfairness, and few, if any, parents will complain. Administrators will recognize that your tests determine how well your students are learning, and they will be able to easily compare the students' performance against the state and school system standards.

Use the Internet to Build Rubrics

Now that you've conquered your fear of technology, you can use it to your advantage once again by visiting a great rubric-creating site: *http://rubistar.4teachers.org*. You can begin creating your own rubrics, projects, papers, and tests after creating an account, which is quick and easy to set up.

These sites provide standard rubric templates for each subject and content area, so you simply customize the rubric to achieve your objective. You also may provide the performance indicators for each objective and the grade to apply to each of these indicators, and then proceed to print out your rubric or test. Remember to provide clear and specific descriptions for each of your criteria so your students will know and understand your expectations. You and your students can clearly measure such things as content, organization, or spelling in order to measure achievement. Use other rubrics as guides by researching them to get ideas. There is really no such thing as a new test, only new testers.

For more information about using and obtaining rubric templates you can go to *http://uen.org/rubric/html/know.html*.

Send the rubric and scoring guide home so parents can discuss them with their child. This way, when the student takes the test, both the student and parents can evaluate his learning. An excellent way to get in contact with parents about the rubrics and tests is through e-mail. Send an e-mail to all the parents with the rubric attached, and e-mail scores to the parents when available. Another Internet option is an online scoring service (my school uses Schoolone.com). Once the test has been taken and scored, you post the scores to your school's site, which can only be accessed by you, the student, and the parent.

There really is no reason in today's Internet world for a parent to suddenly discover when the report card comes out that her student is failing a subject.

Families Without Internet Access

In some school systems, it may be common that families do not have a computer or Internet access available. Therefore, you should survey your class at the beginning of the school year to determine how many students do not have home Internet access. Whenever you send an e-mail update, you should print out the update for those students' parents and mail them to their home addresses.

You can never communicate too frequently with parents. You want them to know they are valued customers.

What Kinds of Tests Are Best?

Are you ready for the answer? The best tests are those that best measure learning. I realize you've already heard it, but here's some further explanation.

Back in my college days we had a theory about our history professor. He gave us those infamous "blue book" tests. His tests consisted of one or two comprehensive questions and we filled the books with everything we could think of that even came close to fitting under the umbrella of an actual response.

We all believed that he graded our tests by standing at the top of a flight of stairs and throwing each blue book down them so the physical weight of our writing became the deciding factor. The books that weighed the most and, therefore, went the farthest got the top grades.

Was there any truth to that being his grading technique? Doubtful. However, what I do know is that our perception of fairness had an important impact on how we studied for his tests. Since we didn't think his tests were fair, we read everything in the textbook covering the area to be tested as well as any outside texts he gave us. We quizzed each other frequently and required in-depth oral responses. I probably learned more history from him than from any other teacher before or after him. Would I have learned so much if he had used the objective true/false or mul-tiple-choice testing? Probably not.

All that said, can you, as an elementary or high school teacher, use such a broad-stroke technique as a test that consists of two open-response questions? Definitely not. Most of your students haven't reached the maturity level for that, nor do they have the innate desire for learning needed to obtain a good assessment using that method. A mixture of objective and comprehensive questioning is your best bet.

Creating the Best Test for Your Students

First of all, you know your students. You know that some of them will always ask before a test how many total questions it will have; if there will be any true/false or multiple-choice questions; and beg that there be no questions requiring them to write and have their writing contain certain specific points or, worse, any logic-based conclusions.

My purpose here isn't to instruct you on the format or content of your testing. You don't fear the actual construction of the test. You're afraid of its ramifications with the students, parents, and administration.

By focusing your tests to cover the content discussed in lessons, lectures, student participative exercises, and class discussions, you have grounded the test and made it fair to all the students in your class. They know what you plan to cover, and as long as you ask questions specific to that content, you cannot be called out for grading your tests by their gross weight. Nor can you be called unfair.

THE FEAR I have spent hours poring over my class lectures, notes, homework assignments, handouts, and quizzes given during a quarter. I write and rewrite quarterly exams and still find that too many of my students fail these. I'm afraid that I'm failing my students.

THE SOLUTION It seems as if you are not paying close enough attention to the questions your students ask during class, or the mistakes made on their quizzes and homework assignments. You need to be sure any missteps are corrected before the final exam, and that special attention is placed on where the majority of those mistakes were made. By getting a better handle on what you need to reteach prior to the final exam, you will be able to gauge what your students have actually learned and what should be covered on your exam.

LET'S SUMMARIZE . . .

❶ Be prepared for your fairness to be questioned.

❷ Use standardized methods of testing to accomplish proper assessment.

❸ There are Internet sources to help develop your rubrics.

❹ Listen to the questions your students ask so you can reteach before an exam.

❺ Communicate your testing rubrics and the results regularly to students, parents, and administrators.

CHAPTER 7

Should I Be Afraid of Being Sued?

Being in charge of a classroom puts you in a tough legal bind. Not only are you accountable for your students' education; you can be held liable if a student injures himself in your classroom. This pertains to both physical and mental injuries. Legal liability issues caused by student injuries include both torts and negligence. Add to those the potential for accusations of criminal acts because you spend your days with minors, and it is no wonder this fear exists.

I spent more than thirty years in the insurance business dealing with issues involving the law and legal liability of both professionals and nonprofessionals, and provided legal liability insurance for lawyers, doctors, nurses, and teachers. Upon entering the teaching profession full-time, I naturally made a point of revisiting the aspects of teacher legal liability with the new perspective of a practicing educator. I do not practice law, but will provide you with some helpful definitions and try to illustrate where you may get into legal trouble. The objective, of course, is to help relieve some of your fears in this area.

The Types of Torts

Tort laws provide protection and resolution for anyone injured by another's unreasonable actions. Claims are legal actions based on state laws that are meant to protect the private rights of individuals.

Intentional Torts

Assault is the most common type of intentional tort. Although no physical contact is required for an assault to exist, since it is an overt attempt to either physically injure a person or create a feeling of fear and an expectation of injury, it is safe to say that the offending person intends to injure the other, thereby fulfilling the definition of an intentional tort. Battery, the other type of intentional tort, results from physical contact.

When you attempt to stop a fight or to discipline a student, make certain to restrain your anger so as not to become involved in potential excessive or cruel punishment with intent to injure the student. Although the courts will take into consideration such things as the student's age, the seriousness of the student's offense, and the student's history of previous conduct, restraining your anger before taking disciplinary action should help keep you out of a situation in which you could be found liable.

Negligence Torts

Unlike intentional torts, a negligence tort means that you neither foresaw nor intended injuries to the other party as a result of your actions. Negligence in a teacher's case requires that she has a duty to protect her students from unreasonable risks, and that failing in her duty caused an actual physical or mental injury to one or more of her students.

A Closer Look

Clearly, you are responsible for the students in your care, and in order to fulfill your duty to protect them from unreasonable risks, you must properly supervise them. Your level of supervision is relative to the level of risk involved in an activity and maintenance of equipment and facilities you use. This duty applies during the school day as well as to activities beyond the school grounds, such as field trips and other co-curricular activities during which the students are in your care.

An element of negligence that is a little more difficult to define involves the legal theory of using a reasonable standard of care. The courts take a number of things into consideration when deciding whether a reasonable standard of care was used, including:

1. How another teacher with similar training and experience would have acted
2. The age of the student
3. The environment in which the incident occurred
4. The type of instructional activity
5. The presence or absence of the supervising teacher
6. The student's disability, if he has one
7. The connection between the teacher's actions or inactions and the student's injury

There are many court cases demonstrating how the courts have ruled in a variety of cases involving allegations of negligence on the part of teachers, administrators, or both. These cases can be used as examples as to the adequate care you must use in handling the students under your supervision. If you have a concern about what that entails in certain situations, discuss it with your appropriate supervisor (your principal, vice principal, or guidance counselor). A physical or mental injury to a child in your care has damaging consequences to several parties, yourself included, so make sure you know the rules and laws in order to protect yourself.

Even if you have a good legal defense of contributory negligence by the student, if you teach or care for students under the age of six, you need to realize that these children have generally been found incapable of contributory negligence.

Liability for Sexual Abuse or Harassment

Again, you need to have a definition of these legal concepts in order to deal with them and lessen your fears in this area.

Quid pro Quo Sexual Harassment: If you explicitly or implicitly make a student's participation in an activity uncomfortable, or make his grade subject to an unwelcome sexual advance, or request sexual favors, or perform any other verbal, nonverbal, or physical action of a sexual nature, you could very likely become guilty of a quid pro quo form of sexual harassment.

A Hostile or Abusive Sexual Environment: If you or a student persists in a harassing behavior to the point that it limits a student's ability to participate or benefit from an education program or activity, your classroom has become a hostile or abusive environment. This one may not seem in your direct control, but as far as the courts are concerned, if it happens, it could be because you failed to perform the appropriate level of supervision over your students.

While you may be quick to dismiss sexual harassment as being something that could not happen in your classroom, you may need to think again. A study titled Sexual Harassment in Education, conducted by Sexual Harassment Support, polled 2,064 students in grades eight through eleven and revealed that 83 percent of girls have been sexually harassed, and 79 percent of boys. So do not be too quick to dismiss this as something that could never happen in your school.

> What on earth does all this mean? It means you must always remember that you are the mature adult with a calm head. Chemical changes in children, especially adolescents and teens, occur sporadically and unpredictably, affecting their reasoning ability, but in the vast majority of cases they will actually listen to you. They take comfort in knowing what to expect from you. Consistency of mature thinking wins the war even though it seems to lose many battles.

There Is Protection Available

In a worst-case scenario, wherein the student's parents take legal action against you, insurance should cover your defense costs and, in certain circumstances, your liability. Most homeowners insurance carriers offer corporal punishment and professional liability coverage to teachers and school administrators for a nominal additional premium. Some will even offer defense-costs coverage for allegations of sexual harassment or abuse, but it only applies if you are found innocent of the charges. Insurance policies in general do not provide coverage for criminal acts; if you were found guilty of sexual harassment or abuse, the insurance would not cover you.

You may also obtain this coverage through the Association of American Educators. This organization, through an arrangement with a specialty insurance broker, offers protection for claims involving allegations of injuries to students under your supervision, failure to educate, violation of a student's rights, failure to promote students or grant credit, improper methods of instruction, and accusations of sexual or physical abuse.

THE FEAR I have a parent who has complained to my principal that I don't teach her child properly because of the distractions of the music I play, or allowing other kids to talk. She says her child needs a quiet environment to focus and learn. I fear legal recriminations on the grounds that I'm not treating everyone equally.

THE SOLUTION Studies have shown that the mind relaxes to music, that it likes repetitive sounds, and that we learn best what we teach. The bigger part of your question, however, is the equal treatment issue. This has become complicated as our society has become more diverse due to racial differences, income level differences, cultural differences, and on, and on. You cannot treat every student exactly the same, but you can make the same learning experience available to every student in your classroom. You must use and document the use of standardized testing, assessment, and curriculum, and apply these with an even temperament. Then communicate these methods to parents, and your administrators.

LET'S SUMMARIZE . . .

❶ There are intentional and unintentional acts that can cause injury, either physical or mental.

❷ If you intentionally harm a student by your actions, whether caused by losing your temper or any other reason, you can be held accountable.

❸ If you do not maintain your professionalism and become negligent, you can unintentionally harm a student and will be held accountable.

❹ Since it is the unintended injury from negligent acts that causes the greatest concern here, you now know that the law defines very precisely a chain of events that leads to you before you can be held accountable.

❺ The special area of sexual actions needs special knowledge and care.

❻ The last resort is insurance protection, which is readily available but has limitations.

CHAPTER 8

I Don't Know If I Can Teach My Subject

It's a great thing to be able to teach a child. And the one-on-one experience is something that both teacher and student will remember forever.

I remember teaching my son how to ride his first two-wheel bicycle. This is the kid who couldn't decide which hand to use to throw a ball and who thought playing the outfield during his first introduction to baseball meant looking for four-leaf clovers.

I must have run a couple of miles back and forth on the sidewalk in front of our house chasing alongside him while he made his first wobbly attempts. There were moments when I thought my exhaustion would win out before his determination would master the skill. I was wrong, and he eventually rode off on his own while I cringed, hoping he wouldn't lose control and fall into the street.

The exercise of teaching this lesson, which required explaining how it all worked (my son had to know all the mechanical details of everything before he would venture forth), and then going from walking along holding the handlebars to actually just doing a small bit of balancing to help him charge off on his own, gave me my first lesson in teaching. I knew how to ride a bike. I knew how the bicycle was put together. I knew how to fix it when it broke. The one thing I didn't know was how to explain balance. Doesn't that just come naturally? Then how do I explain it? It took a lot of time, but I was able to get the principle across through action, example, and explanation. My son soon was riding the bike by himself.

The good thing was that it was just the two of us. What if I had tried to teach that lesson to several kids all at once? How about thirty? Feel that tingle of fear creeping up your back as you think about that?

Your Major Could Be Their Minor

Recently, it's been said that we should not teach what we learned most easily because we would have trouble understanding a student's difficulty in learning the subject. This doesn't mean, however, that you shouldn't know your subject. For example, just the other day in my public speaking class I began my section on debating. I told the class that our debates would be conducted in teams, and we would pick our topics from those suggested by the National Forensic League.

They reacted by quickly choosing teams based on friendships. I followed my comments by saying that they should consider debate team selection in a different light from selection of friends. We pick our friends because friends tend to think alike. When it comes to debating, the team that has members who are both for and against a debate topic will have the best chance of winning. The team who has such members will know how the opposition thinks, giving it a definite advantage, just like a football team with a defensive squad that reads the offense's plays well.

If you have learned your subject by questioning its premises, then you will have prepared yourself for the questions that your students will have and can prepare your presentations of the material accordingly.

Has Your Subject Changed? Fear Not; It Has.

Of course the subject you are teaching has changed over the years. As time goes on, the understanding of each subject has evolved, and teachers are expected to keep up with these subject evolutions. Following is a quick recap by department as to how each subject has changed over the years:

- Science goes without question, even if you teach elementary school. In the last few decades, we've expanded our knowledge of the universe, visited Mars by way of robotic rovers, and seen the birth of stars using hyperspeed, deep-space telescopes. In addition, Mendeleev's original periodic table of elements has grown, and continues to grow, and the body of knowledge generated by medical and environmental research expands daily.

- Has language, grammar, or style changed? It sure has. With the dependence on online communication, we've seen new words come into use, many grammar rules relaxed, and a whole new text-message language created, although it's still not acceptable in the classroom.

- Mathematics has expanded beyond mathematicians' chalkboards as it's entered the field of criminal investigation and placed statistical analysis tools in the hands of businesspeople.

- The visual and written arts have always reflected the sociopolitical world and still do. Now, both have the support of computerized programs that speed up the artistic process fantastically.

■ And while history never changes, our interpretation does, based on our perception of it and how the perception applies to modern-day events. Just look at all the different views of Americans' right to free speech or to bear arms.

The Change to Kinesthetic and Visual Learning

The way kids learn has not really changed at all over the years. Children have always learned most easily when they can see a concept in action and put their hands on it (as in the bike lessons I gave). Remember how you learned to drive, or hit a tennis ball. You got behind the wheel with your instructor sitting close by and drove away. You kept hitting tennis balls until they not only went over the net, but went there with the speed you wanted and landed where you wanted. You did these things after some verbal instruction, but the majority of learning came behind the wheel or with racket in hand.

Hands-on instruction now takes the form of student interaction using Smart Boards, computers, calculators, and group problem-solving. There are statistics verifying that learning occurs best when something is being taught to another, rather than just being read in a book or listened to in discussion. And so, as a teacher today you must use as many techniques as you can to put your students in the driver's seat, no matter how many students you have in the classroom.

But There Are So Many Students

Your worry that you can't really teach in a room of thirty or more kids is well-founded. However, this worry translates into fear, and your fear becomes an obstacle to your teaching. In order to overcome this fear, you must be confident that you can teach the subject you are in charge of teaching, and you can do so in an authoritative yet approachable manner. As long as you have control over your class and your students, you will be able to give each of them the individual attention they need.

Don't forget that you are the only person in the room who has experienced childhood, adolescence, and adulthood. The more kids you have in your room, the more chances you have to assist America in having a future that promotes freedom and democracy. Learn as much as you can about each student, and do this as early in the school year as possible. You will find the ways they learn best. Recognizing each student as an individual learner and knowing the ways in which you can assist each child in her education will ultimately make your classroom experience better for everyone, students and teacher alike. (Check out Chapters 9 and 15 to learn more about handling diversity in your classroom.)

THE FEAR I teach United States History to 150 freshmen. I get that many or more new faces and personalities each year. I start the year with the landing of Columbus and am nearly to the Civil War before I even know all their names. I don't have time to read and grade essay-length papers, so all my tests are objective. I have become more and more frustrated, because it seems like every time I watch the news or go out to places where adults congregate, I hear that no one knows any of our valuable history, let alone understands the significance of it to our generation. I just have too many kids to teach well.

THE SOLUTION Kids at that age have one primary interest: friends. They don't seem to care about anything that isn't popular right now.

So, you need to make history happen. When was the last time you read a historical novel or saw a history-based movie? Have you ever asked a student to talk to his or her grandparents about what things were like during their early years? Kids love their grandparents, and grandparents love telling those kinds of stories. If you can get these kinds of conversations going at home, you will be amazed at how the kid becomes a teacher when retelling the grandparents' story to the rest of the class, and how interested they are in the time period when their grandparents grew up. Capturing student interest in your subject will captivate the class and allow for a better learning environment.

LET'S SUMMARIZE . . .

❶ Fear not the depth of your knowledge of a subject, for yours is the only expertise in the classroom.

❷ Diversity within your classroom is not a drawback to the learning that takes place there; rather, it enhances it.

❸ You became a teacher because you like learning, so don't stop. You have learning thrown at you every day. It comes in the mail, from other teachers, and, most important, from your students.

❹ Student learning hasn't really changed with the advent of the computer and digitization of the world. Learning is like matter in that it can't be created or destroyed; it just changes form. Tell them, show them, and then let them work with it. Your fear about lack of subject knowledge and the size of your class will melt away as you see and hear the results of focusing on the learning going on, and not on your teaching.

PART II

Student Fears

So many kids, so many things that could

go wrong

———————

———————

———————

CHAPTER 9

Are My Students Bored?

"That makes like no sense!"

"I won't ever need that. No one I know actually uses algebra. Why are we studying that?"

"I don't ever plan to be a writer, so why are we spending time on poetry? Ugh!"

Ever hear these questions or comments? Sure you have. Other students just think these things and either put their heads on their desks, feigning sleep, or simply stare in your direction. Unfortunately, the only thing on their minds is hoping the bell will ring soon so they can go to lunch, or basketball practice, or get home to their video games. The reasons for these mind-wanderings are as various as the number of students participating in them. They see no connection between the class and what they consider real life, or don't understand the subject matter, or find understanding the subject matter so easy they allow their minds to seek other interesting things.

I have a student in my general business class who loves "hot" cars. I had given the class an assignment to review various aspects of some major corporations that were found to qualify as "Innovators" by *BusinessWeek* magazine. He quite naturally wanted to research BMW. It didn't actually qualify based on *BusinessWeek's* criteria, but since I knew of his high level of interest in cars, and his low level of grades in nearly every subject, I agreed. While he and the other students worked on their research using the computers in my classroom, I wandered around observing their progress, helping with problems. When I stopped to see how this student was doing, he excitedly asked me if I knew the differential ratio in a BMW. (This is the ratio of the number of times the drive shaft turns to the turns of the rear wheels through the gears in the differential box.) I told him I didn't, and we got into a discussion of these ratios in relation to the torque and horsepower developed at certain RPMs (revolutions per minute of the crankshaft). This young man had an excellent grasp of these concepts but was failing algebra, and had told his algebra teacher he saw no relevance to it. What was he (and we teachers) missing?

In my business class we also spent some time with the simple math calculations needed to figure things like break-even and market share. Until we began working with real examples from their lives, such as estimating Levi's share of the jeans market, or Motorola's share of the cell phone business, they saw no point. One student even asked why he had to do such things in business class since he had already done them in math class. I took the opportunity to explain the relevance.

Bring outside businesspeople into your classroom wherever possible, or take short field trips to see the operation of businesses. I have the fortunate situation of having experienced more than thirty years in corporate America, and so have lots of real-life stories to share with my students. If your students saw a newspaper printing operation running almost entirely by computers, they would not only be fascinated, but would see geometry, algebra, language arts, fine arts, and engineering in action.

The only real-world work experience many of them get involves part-time work in the fast-food industry, and they don't realize all the complicated efforts involved even in that. All they know is they go in to work, and learn how to operate a computerized cash register. They don't have to learn how to make change, calculate inventory usage, order supplies of food, understand how the temperature of the cooking facilities must be precise for consistent results, and learn why certain prices are charged for all the different products and combinations of sizes and products. All these things and more are done by a computer system.

When you discover you have a student who works in one of these establishments, ask him to do some research while working. Ask how many burgers were sold along with French fries and a soft drink during his shift. Or, ask how much cash he took in compared to how much the total intake was during his shift. Ask what the temperature of the cooking facilities was, and why. Ask how long it took to cook a burger and how many could be cooked at one time.

Ask any students who baby-sit how much they make per hour. Then ask how much they would have to charge to make a profit if they had to buy the diapers, baby food, lotions, and a toy or two during their time taking care of the infant.

These correlations between the subjects they learn in school and their outside lives will make them appreciate what they are learning in school, and how they can use what they are learning to better their outside lives.

Do You Bore Them?

When is the last time you recorded yourself during class? If you have never done this, I strongly suggest you do so. You may speak so softly the kids in the back of the room can't hear you. You may constantly repeat certain phrases, causing them to lose any significance. You may discover you failed to talk about something significant. But, most important, you may lack enthusiasm. Without enthusiasm, the best possible message will fall on deaf ears. With enthusiasm you can sell ice to an Eskimo.

If you don't feel passionate about your message, you have no message. Remember, Zig Ziglar says, "we are what goes into our minds." If you tell yourself that all you want is to coast until retirement, you will coast. If you tell yourself that it doesn't matter how you deliver your material and that this lazy bunch of kids will never get it, they won't get it.

I attended a motivational seminar a few years ago. Ziglar was the main speaker, and he told an interesting story. He said he and friends were having dinner at a nice restaurant one evening and noticed that the waiter apparently didn't like his job. He took their orders without suggestions, and simply delivered the food when it came to him from the kitchen. Zig says he had to ask the waiter for a dessert menu when they had finished their main course, and had to ask for more coffee when their cups were empty. He emphasized to the audience that this was an upscale restaurant that charged upscale prices. So, when the waiter arrived with their check, Zig asked him if he liked his job, obviously knowing the answer. When the waiter said that he hated his job, Zig told him not to worry, he wouldn't have it long.

You have the future of this great country in your hands. Don't blow it. The subject matter you teach, whether it's the basics of the alphabet or the details of calculus, forms the basis for future brain surgeons, engineers, and, yes, even teachers.

Working with Diversity

If you have more than two students in your room, you have the potential for diversity of learning styles. What will excite one may actually seem irrelevant or boring to another. The days of a teacher standing in front of twenty well-behaved kids, lecturing while they diligently take notes and ensuring that they score well enough on standardized tests to keep the principal off their back, are over. The No Child Left Behind, modern-day governmental approach to education forces you to find ways for all the divergent personalities in your classroom to learn at least enough to pass the state-mandated tests.

Do you ever wonder why the children of today have so many different learning styles? Are we doing something as a society to cause ADD, ADHD, autism, and Asperger's syndrome, or has the human gene pool simply mutated through an inevitable evolution of man?

Understanding Diversity

I believe that understanding diversity in as much depth as possible will add to your teaching skills. Spending a portion of your summer reading up on these areas of psychology, taking summer college courses, and attending seminars where these issues are discussed should become a part of your continuing education.

You are not alone in your fear of diversity in learning styles, and should take comfort in that. Knowing you will have kids in your classroom who have a great deal of difficulty focusing, or in understanding anything figurative or conceptual, arms you with the desire to educate yourself further on how to present your subject matter so these students will learn from you.

Dr. David Vawter has a wonderful seminar on diversity through the Bureau of Education & Research. If you can't get away to attend one of these seminars, you can purchase the recordings of them and listen to them, as I have done, during your morning commute.

You know you will have students who fail to do homework, forget to bring their book to class, and don't listen well while you're teaching. Discover who they are early in the school year. Their teachers from the previous grade will provide invaluable insight into this. Ask them.

I currently use an assignment table for my junior-level remedial English class. Each student has a blue card with his or her name on it. Under this card I have placed a series of assignments based on the student's ability level and the goals I have established for the individual's growth through the quarter. I roam the room as they work on their assignments to see how they are doing, and help where needed. Some are reading from the assigned novel. Some are reading and answering questions from an assignment book. Some are reading stories from a *Reader's Digest* magazine (like most newspapers, it is written to the sixth-grade reading level) and writing down any words they don't understand so they can look them up in the dictionary and then write a sentence using them. Some are doing a writing assignment using a computer.

Ultimately, all assignments have a written component, which the students will work on using Microsoft Word. They then send the assignments to me as an e-mail attachment. I read each attachment and make editorial corrections using the Track Changes option in Word (a program function that lets viewers see what was changed), give it a grade, and send it back. Any assignment that focuses on writing, whether a paragraph or an essay, can be rewritten by the student and sent back to me as many times as desired, until the student has an excellent paper. The students keep all the edited copies in a file for reference when writing new papers. That way they learn from their own mistakes.

You may also want to use an Internet source at *www.turnitin .com*. It is a tremendous way to gain help in checking not only grammar but in checking for plagiarism and copying from another of your student's paper.

No system is perfect, and diversity of learning styles certainly challenges the most out-of-the-box-thinking teacher, but if you give it a good effort the kids will benefit and your fears in this area will diminish greatly.

THE FEAR I have a classroom with tables that can accommodate as many as six students. It's great for my students when working on a group project, but I really have a tough time getting them to stop chatting or passing notes when I'm talking. How am I supposed to gain their attention when I lecture?

THE SOLUTION Recently, I attended a seminar that introduced the learning power of music. You can use it to excite, to encourage, to calm, and to reinforce learning and memory. Children from kindergarten through twelfth grade love music. As they reach the upper teens and find a way to acquire iPods or headsets and any other means of bringing music into their lives, they do it. Why not use that in your classroom? Use the exciting beat of *The Crazy Frogs* as students come into your room. If it is the first thing in the morning, they will come out of their morning fog, or funk, as the case may be. If it's the last class of the day, this type of upbeat music will enliven their spirits.

When you read to them or go over information they need to commit to memory, play a Miles Davis jazz CD. When you have an activity that gets them on their feet, play something from a Ray Lynch CD that has a synthesized upbeat tempo. When you want them to stop an activity, stop the music. They will instantly stop what they are doing and look at you. They aren't looking at you because you have created automatons, but because they wonder why the music stopped. Just don't play music with words because they will begin singing to it, at least in their minds, and you will not have their undivided attention.

One other thing you can do, if you know that an element of your lesson plan will require you to lecture, is to do the lecture first. Arrange the tables in a V or U shape around the room while you play the music. Then turn the music down or off and stand or walk around in the middle of the space and outside the tables while lecturing. If you want them all to look at the whiteboard or Smart Board, have their chairs all turned in that direction. After the first time or two of this arrangement they will get it and not move the chairs to face the tables until after you finish lecturing. Oh, and keep the lectures short.

LET'S SUMMARIZE . . .

❶ Help your students find the relevance in your subject.

❷ Know the interests of your students.

❸ Today's children have many issues, making their learning styles different. Educate yourself so you will know how to develop learning in all your students.

❹ Remember that some students will appear bored even when they are learning.

CHAPTER 10

Why Won't These Kids Let Me Teach Them?

You will have students who will be determined not to learn from you. Do you give up? Certainly not, but recognizing this fact will allow you to focus on the learning that takes place in the minds of the rest of the students in your classroom. This chapter will help you understand the motivations behind students' deliberately closing their minds to knowledge.

Don't Confuse Unwillingness to Learn with Failing Grades

You probably have, or have had, students who did enough to pass your class but who allowed nothing to enter their long-term memory. You recognized them by their apparent inability to make connections or understand concepts. Here are some reasons why that could occur:

1. There may be cultural differences based on where and how they were raised by their families. Your students may live in a part of the community that is totally foreign to your experience of growing up. Your students may be from a lower or higher social class than you are, which in either

case can cause difficulty in getting your lessons across to the students.

2. Your students may be letting their personal pride get in the way of their education. They cannot appear to learn what you have to teach because it would go against the persona they have built for themselves. This form of reasoning will contradict everything you know. After all, you love learning. That's why you became a teacher. But you need to forget the way you have been approaching education.

> The bully becomes the bully for many reasons; the class clown becomes the class clown for many reasons; the student who chooses not to learn becomes the student who chooses not to learn for many reasons. No matter the reason, these stereotypes have created an identity the students must cling to for all they are worth. That is the point. This label has become their reality, overcoming whatever fear of normal life they brought to school.

3. Today's American classroom is filled with a number of students who speak English as their second language. As the "great melting pot," the United States has a storied history of immigration. Some of the immigrants actually came to America speaking English, but most did not. The earlier waves of immigrants were forced to conform and speak English; however, with the latest waves, the call to conform has not been as strong because it's now recognized that language is part of the immigrant culture. This creates difficulty for teachers who must instruct students in English, even though that might not be the language spoken at home.

4. Often, students' personal experiences and past history get in the way of their learning. Trying to teach someone to unlearn personal experience is extremely difficult, as it's

basically on par with erasing memories. A student may feel that he has given math his best shot, but still fails. As his teacher you now have to overcome his past failures in order to teach him math. Each student's actions are influenced by unique educational experiences.

5. Once a teenage student is set in her ways, she will use her unbelievably strong willpower to remain in those ways. I spent many years in corporate America and was amazed at some of the corporate leaders' strength of will. They went against tremendous odds, and would get their way. Now that I teach teenagers, I have to say their will to get their way far exceeds anything I encountered in the business world. Because they lack a true understanding of the long-term implications of their current actions, teenagers will hold steadfast in their way.

6. Ever heard a student say, "No way I can learn that"? Whether spoken by a first-grader or twelfth-grader, those words can get under any teacher's skin. However, it may not be the student's fault that he says this. When given certain information from an authority figure often enough, he not only believes it; it becomes a part of him. If a parent has decided her child can't learn because she had difficulty teaching him during his preschool years, or some misguided professional counselor has advised the parent that her child couldn't learn easily, or a teacher told the child he was stupid, the child believes he is stupid.

7. Some students have just lost hope. If you have a student who has lost hope in herself, she may linger in the back of the room after others have left. Or, she may just as easily appear normal, moving with, but just behind, the crowd. She hasn't been told she is stupid, and isn't necessarily a bad kid; she just has no hope for her future because she has no faith in

herself. Hopeless adolescents' minds have become so riddled with sources of hopelessness that they cannot learn from you or any other teacher until they overcome the problem.

These seven points only brush the surface, but they are broad enough to cover the main reasons why a student may not be responding to your teaching.

How to Handle "Lost" Students

I had a conversation recently with one of my better students because he was obviously flustered. He said his workload had him so overwhelmed he didn't know what to do next. As we talked, I calmly and quietly asked him questions about his assignments. Talking about it seemed to help him, so I asked him to take a blank sheet of paper and write whatever came to his mind. I emphasized that he not try to place any priority on anything, or to create a numbered list, but to just write randomly. (I know from personal experience that when I finish doing this I feel tremendous relief.)

I wrote a note to the teacher of his next class explaining the reason for his tardiness and gave it to him. I told him that my next period was for planning so we wouldn't be interrupted. He agonized over the first items he wrote but completed his list in a few minutes, sat back, and I could see the tension leave his body as he read the list. Next I asked him to prioritize the items from the most to the least important. He did this, exhaled, got up, picked up his books, his list, smiled at me, and left.

The human mind is complex. Students who choose not to learn from you are going through some complex issues. If you take a minute to help simplify these issues, you will have a better chance of getting through to the students when you are in front of the class.

THE FEAR No matter what I do, I cannot seem to get through to several of my students because of my Jewish religion. I know this group believes in the "Aryan Brotherhood," and they frighten me. I weigh all my teaching commentary before I speak so as not to have any implication of teaching Judaism. How do I teach them anything?

THE SOLUTION You now fear not only the students, but yourself. You must overcome both. Start with your fear of yourself. You have a personal perspective that has become a part of you. Embrace it but don't flaunt it. In other words, focus on the lesson you want the students to learn, not on whether your delivery has a Jewish bias. Hold on to the knowledge that you know the subject and that you must impart your knowledge in the best way you know how. If you somehow find yourself saying something that your internal voice says is a Jewish thought, and this will happen, stay on the subject. The students, no matter their age, will recognize hypocrisy in teachers who hide themselves quicker than most adults will. And with students, hypocrisy means you are not trustworthy, and so no learning takes place. Which is worse: measuring every word so as not to offend a few but alienating the majority, or teaching the best way you know how at the risk of alienating a few who only appear not to be learning from you? Remember, a failing grade on a report card doesn't necessarily mean no learning occurred.

LET'S SUMMARIZE . . .

❶ Many students won't learn from you, and you don't know why.

❷ Knowledge will bring solutions.

❸ There are several reasons for the apparent lack of learning: loyalties, integrity, identity, language, personal experience, struggle of wills, learned stupidity, and hopelessness.

❹ The complexities of the human mind seem endless, so you must continue in your pursuit of understanding.

CHAPTER 11

How Do I Deal with Harassing Students?

Will racial slurs ever stop? As long as ignorance and prejudice exist, racial slurs and epithets will continue. Parental misguidance and peer pressure have a strong control over a juvenile's actions, and his use of racial slurs in your classroom may be a result of those outside influences. However, you do have a tremendous influence over your students and can use that influence to try to undo any negative predispositions.

Much of the time you may feel you are fighting an uphill battle, but whatever you do, don't give up. If you fear these comments in your classroom, and don't know what you should do when you hear them, just remember that your classroom is a microcosm of the larger society. If you do not want this type of hate speech happening in society, you need to stop it in your classroom.

You must make certain to eliminate any prejudice from your classroom. The moment the kids walk into your room, they must know you require the use of proper English with zero tolerance for racial slurs. If you routinely use certain racially prejudicial phrases outside your classroom, say among friends, you must stop. If you use these at all, you will accidentally use them or some variation of them while teaching, and you will destroy whatever else you have done to rid your students of their prejudice.

Racism Within the Race

You also need to realize that racism can be perpetuated within a race and doesn't necessarily need to be between people of different races. It may take on different forms represented by different words, or the same words used by different people. Just because a derogatory term for black people comes out of the mouth of a black child and is directed toward another black child doesn't mean that the word isn't degrading, insulting, or reflecting intolerance. The same is true when a Hispanic, Asian, or Caucasian student insults another student of the same race with a racist or derogatory term. It doesn't matter who the intended party is; it just matters that the term is being used and the hate is being perpetuated.

Children and Racism

You have heard and will hear many other words with dehumanizing characteristics used by children of almost all ages. Whether the child knows the full meaning and hurtful nature of the words, or whether you know them, doesn't matter; you must not allow their use in your classroom. The kids will adapt. You must convey to them that using offensive words affects all who hear them. What you instill in their minds will help shape who they become.

A very simple example of this occurred to me during my childhood years. I used to spend a couple of weeks in the summer with my grandparents, helping out on their farm in southeastern Kentucky. Upon my return, my friends all made fun of my "hillbilly" accent and I truly understood how cruel kids can be. That hurt, and until they did this, I was unaware that I picked up those speech patterns, and of the prejudice of my friends. I knew my grandparents spoke differently, but I also thought their unique expressions sounded cool.

My two weeks of immersion in the Kentucky hill country each summer changed not only my way of speaking, but my way of thinking. I developed a healthy respect for their way of life. My grandparents and the local community had a strong moral base and a firm grasp on logic. Sure, many of them had little formal education, but all of them could detect a fake a mile away.

My point here is simple: Kids can't appreciate what they don't know. They have trouble understanding a way of life outside of their own, whether that view appears obvious because of skin color or not. You should not fear making them aware of this. They will respect you for it even if they don't show it.

> You need to use whatever method you can to make sure the students in your classroom understand that they are in a learning environment and that intolerance will not be tolerated. They watch everything you do and listen to everything you say. They need to know that you too watch and listen to their whole person.

Homophobic Students

You must have a holistic understanding of your students. However, your students have yet to fully identify themselves, so you must be open to the young people they are becoming. While you may be able to easily identify racial prejudices, you may not be able to detect any issues your students are facing due to homosexuality.

The truly heartbreaking thing about homosexuality is the apparent invisibility that exacerbates the identity crisis every teen faces. Even those teens living in functional homes will have problems coming to terms with themselves and their families. The potential psychological damage is incalculable.

You, as an educator, must remain vigilant to your students' lives so as to ascertain when any student has become the target of homophobic slurs. Simple effeminate actions by a boy could cause him to become the unfortunate recipient of harmful name-calling. You must overcome any fear you may have of dealing directly with this issue. It won't go away, and a child's life hangs in the balance.

THE FEAR I have a seventeen-year-old girl in my class who is openly gay. I saw her attempting to embrace another girl, whose body language told me she did not welcome it. I quietly intervened. Now the gay girl frequents my classroom after school, always taking a desk next to mine. She has no misunderstanding about my sexuality. I am happily married with two small children. Since my desk can't be seen from the hallway even with the door open, rumors have begun to circulate through the student body that she and I are having a lesbian love affair. Kids really are cruel.

THE SOLUTION You certainly are right about the cruel part. I suggest you do three things. First of all, get a couple of students to move your desk so that anyone in the hallway can clearly see you and anyone sitting next to you. Second, I would let the guidance counselor know by personal visit and follow-up e-mail or other written documentation just what you did to help the student who did not consent, and that you have frequent visits from the gay student. And finally, I would pay particular attention to the subject matter of the discussions brought to you by the gay student. If you feel she is now making incorrect advances toward you, it is time to involve the counselor and parents. If she is making idle chit-chat, you need to decide whether or not it's because she has no other friends. Either way, you always need to be friendly to your students, but you cannot and must not be their friend. Keep it on the teacher–student level or you're playing with dynamite.

LET'S SUMMARIZE . . .

❶ The use of racial slurs has many underlying causes. Learn and understand them and do not tolerate them.

❷ The use of homophobic slurs has many causes. Make sure you continue educating yourself as to the potential causes.

❸ Remain aware of the needs of the victims in either case.

CHAPTER 12

What If a Student Has a Medical Emergency?

Death affects everyone and strikes fear in all. As a teacher, you bring not only the fear of your own death occurring in the classroom, but also that of one of your students passing away in the presence of you and your other students.

The occurrence of an adolescent's death takes on a special meaning, whether preceded by illness or not. We naturally expect those in their advanced years to die while we still live. After all, adults all know that death is inevitable. We do not expect, however, to bury our children, nor do we expect the young to die unless they have a terminal illness.

> If you dwell on the potential of a student's sudden illness or death happening in your classroom, you should seek advice from a professional qualified to help you. If you simply have a natural fear of it happening, you need to know how to handle it.

Students and Illness

If you have doubts as to the sincerity of an illness professed by a student, send him to the school nurse. One of the skills you learn very quickly in working with children all day is how to detect a real illness from an I-just-want-to-get-out-of-class illness. You even learn which students to suspect. The real fear occurs when a student you don't expect to lie about an illness suddenly vomits. Or, worse yet, when you look up from the book you are discussing and see a student suddenly drop her head to the desk or fall to the floor, having lost consciousness.

Sure, you have latex gloves, hand disinfectant, bandages, and other first-aid implements in your desk drawer for a reason, but you never actually thought you would need them. Then it happens. When it does, make sure you have read and understood the school preparedness actions you need to take to reduce further injury to that student and to prevent a spread of the illness or injury to other classmates. As in anything else, being prepared reduces fear.

Take for Example . . .

I read a story recently about a teacher who was distracted by a serious illness in her family. She gave her students an assignment. They went to work and she took out her cell phone and called the hospital for an update. As she looked away for those few moments, one student handed another a candy bar. The receiving student took a bite and in seconds went into anaphylactic shock, fell to the floor, and died. The candy bar contained peanuts, to which the student was highly allergic.

I tell you this not to frighten you but to make a point. Children do not know the consequences of their actions; no matter how many times someone tells them. Should the teacher not have made that call? Could she have stopped the candy offer if she hadn't lost her focus? No one knows the answers to those questions. All that's known is that a child died. An already worried teacher just became a distraught one.

Should you live in fear of that happening in your classroom? No. You should not live that way. What you should do, however, is take time off from school when personal events take away your ability to concentrate. Your students will learn more once you come back, your classroom will be a safer place, and you will be ready to get back into the swing of things.

A Student Faints or Loses Consciousness

You need to be able to act quickly in the case of a loss of consciousness in your classroom, and the injuries that can result. Bruises, broken bones, and blood loss each need special treatment beyond the scope of the first aid you know. Your fear of causing further injury by not responding correctly makes you take careful steps when an emergency like this happens. Embrace that fear. It will mean you react in a way that will benefit the injured student, and at the same time, protect the other students from harm.

This book is not meant to provide you with medical training, but only with knowledge that will help dispel your fears. Keep your first-aid gear and any school manual at the ready, and be prepared to use them.

In many cases, your school's medical response team will be able to handle an emergency that happens in your classroom. However, there may be a time when the emergency will be too much to handle and the student's life cannot be saved.

Sudden Death in the Classroom

Hypertrophic cardiomyopathy (an enlargement of the heart), congenital coronary artery anomalies (abnormal blood vessels around the heart), aortic stenosis (narrowing of the aorta), dysrhythmias (abnormal cardiac rhythms), and Marfan syndrome (a connective tissue disorder) are some of the more common causes of sudden adolescent death.

The enlarged heart usually refers to an enlarged left ventricle blocking the blood flow, thus causing abnormal heart rhythms (arrhythmia). Death from this cause typically occurs in the teenage athlete during exercise. The athlete may have ignored warning symptoms, or assumed they were just due to overexertion.

You should not have to worry about this happening in your classroom, unlike the previously mentioned case of a reaction to a peanut allergy. However, as always, knowledge of what to do in the case of a cardiac emergency or otherwise should reduce any fear.

The statistics weigh heavily in favor of your never having to face such an event. Knowing what to do if it does occur will be part of your school manual. However, it never hurts to have some helpful tips.

Be Prepared

First of all, your school should have a Public Access Defibrillation Program and an automated type of defibrillator (AED). The school would typically keep it near or in a gymnasium, the location of most athletic events. The plan should include instruction in the use of the AED by a core emergency response team of trained personnel, and a method to communicate with and activate the team. If you are unsure of your school's plan, or even whether your school has one in place, you should speak to an administrator. The school should also have a follow-up plan in the case of a student death.

Handling a Student's Death

The emergency doesn't end with the death. The need for others to heal begins immediately and generally includes the emotions of denial and isolation, anger, bargaining, depression, and finally acceptance. This will happen with the student body as well as the faculty. These emotions among the students may switch swiftly, so you will need to encourage them to express their emotions, without pushing them to the extremes of rage or self-destructive behavior.

During the recovery process, each member of the faculty has a role. Such things as emptying the deceased student's locker, pulling a cumulative folder, identifying a central area within the school for support or counseling, and making announcements over the internal P.A. system and to the media should be left to the individuals previously appointed to the tasks. After the funeral, the principal should thank everyone for all the support, and announce that guidance staff will remain available should anyone wish to talk to a counselor.

During all these events, you should make certain not to miss any all-staff meetings. You also should allow for all expressions of grief and for discussions of students' fears, as well as talk about the funeral. If appropriate, you should attend the funeral yourself. If the death occurred by suicide, emphasize that suicide is an error in judgment, a tragically permanent solution to temporary problems. Send any apparent high-risk students to the guidance office, or channel their names to a counselor. Finally, don't forget fellow faculty members who may need a good listener.

Helping Your Students Through a Classmate's Death

The grieving process does not always have the specific stages as mentioned, so pay particular attention to the possibility of a student having a powerful feeling of anger or guilt later on.

While you need to listen well, during this period you also must not make promises you can't keep. The child needs to know that you will do what you say, especially while he or she is questioning the very basis of life. Watch for crying and/or sobbing, anxiety, headaches, abdominal pain, hostile reactions toward the deceased, failure to complete homework, poor grades, lack of attention and concentration, loss of manual skills, and fear of maintaining friendships.

A high-risk person may be identified by these characteristics:

- Participated in any way in a suicide or accident
- Knew of the suicide attempt and didn't try to stop it
- Feels guilty about things said to the deceased prior to the death
- Recently punished or threatened to punish the deceased
- Did not take the suicide threat seriously
- Was too busy to talk to the deceased, who asked for help
- Is a relative, best friend, or self-appointed therapist
- Identifies with the victim's situation
- Has a history of suicidal threats or attempts or, in desperation, now considers suicide a viable alternative

Suicidal death is much different from any death from natural causes and must be handled carefully. Do not glorify the act of suicide. Do not make an announcement of death by suicide if you have the assignment of making public statements. Recognize the tragedy of the event by acknowledging the various reactions to it. Any memorials should focus on coping with life's struggles and on living, such as planting a tree or making donations to a crisis hotline. Return to normal school activities as soon as possible.

Every event involving death in a school community has as many different complications as there are people. We are creatures with a complexity of emotions that this book cannot fully or appropriately address; just know that you are one of those human beings.

THE FEAR I have a student in a wheelchair and another with an implanted dialysis pump. I know that the child in the wheelchair suffered from a birth defect, leaving her paralyzed from the waist down. As for the other student, I don't feel I know enough about diabetes to deal with that. What should I do?

THE SOLUTION Part of the solution to both of these is to learn more about each situation. Talk to the parents to let them know of your concerns. If nothing else, they will appreciate your concern for taking care of their child. One other important thing you should do is discuss these students with the school nurse, who will let you know what to do if the students need your help. You do not have to have the knowledge of a medical professional, and should make no attempt to give any medical advice to these or any of your students.

LET'S SUMMARIZE . . .

❶ Students will enter your classroom ill or will become ill while there. Make sure you have the proper first-aid knowledge and equipment.

❷ If a student faints and falls, make sure you look for injuries that may have occurred. Calm the other students and contact the office or nurse as quickly as possible.

❸ The potential of a student dying in your classroom can create a nightmare unless you properly prepare. You know that handling a natural death requires actions different from those of a suicide. Make sure you attend all required staff meetings following the death of a student, and that you take the follow-up steps needed to assuage the feelings of the rest of your students.

CHAPTER 13

How Do I Handle Fear of the Bullies?

There exist in this world bullies who use many forms of physical and emotional violence toward their victims as well as their victims' families and friends. They use embarrassment, shame, bodily injury, digital harassment, and many other ways to strike fear into the hearts of those around them. Their reasons are many and varied. Their victims' fears affect you, your classroom, and your school. Although the bully's issues actually begin somewhere in his home, they start affecting you as soon as the kids get off the morning school bus. In order to end the fear in your classroom, you have to identify the victims so that you may get help for them.

> The fear of violence will not go away entirely by your knowing how to recognize and handle bullying, but it should diminish to a level that allows calm, deliberate action when needed.

Although the National Center for Education Statistics has done surveys of the frequency of bullying and the types of forms it takes, many victims don't report it. Suffice to say that even if no one in your classroom complains about bullying, with eighty-one percent of public schools reporting some form of violence, you need to prepare yourself.

How Do I Recognize the Victims?

Your fear of not recognizing the victims heightens as you watch the children descending from the school bus steps, because you do not have most of them in your classroom. You recognize them just as you recognize the neighbors with whom you've never spoken, but who always smile and wave if you see them out mowing their lawn or driving past your home. You recognize the children from walking the hallways to class or outside for a fire drill, or playing on the school playground. But you don't really know them, and you only have limited contact with them during bus, hall, or lunch duty. So how do you recognize whether they are victims of bullying?

Immediate signs of physical violence, such as a bloody nose, black eye, or broken glasses, are obvious. The victims will do their best to conceal evidence of emotional harm out of fear of reprisals beyond those actually threatened by the bully. The sinister nature of bullying can cause irreparable damage to a child's feeling of self-worth that will stay with him for a lifetime. Some day, if you have done a good job of educating the future citizenry of this nation, each of them will look for gainful employment, have great friendships, or love another person enough to want to spend their lives together. A student who is a victim of bullying may find it very difficult, if not impossible, to make these choices. So you watch them. Watch and listen to them as they talk with their friends. Pay close attention to any serious changes in those relationships.

According to the National Center for Education Statistics, bullies operate more effectively in the elementary school age groups than in high school, but they do operate in both. So, when the kids descend those school bus steps, walk the halls, or eat their lunches, pay close attention to their friendly banter. Look at faces and you will find that most reflect a healthy attitude, a smile (except in the teenage years when sleepiness or peer pressure to appear bored overcomes them), and even some laughter. Once students have cleared the bus or cafeteria lines, talk with the driver or cafeteria workers. Most conscientious school professionals know the normal interaction of their kids, and this quick conversation will offer them an opportunity to share any concerns that may have developed that day. Remember, even though they aren't professional teachers or child psychologists, they may have important observational abilities. Many have children of their own and have developed that parental sixth sense.

What Makes a Bully a Bully?

Most bullies have a home life that you would not wish on your most fearsome student. They often live in fear themselves. They feel no self-worth and strive for attention or the love they do not feel from parents. They see how quickly inflicting harm gets attention, even if it's not the loving attention they want. They do not understand their need for love that's expressed by closeness and understanding; they just know they have to inflict fear to gain the attention equated with love. They slap the small, unathletic boy as he passes them to take his seat on the bus, or take the younger girl's lunch, and threaten to kill her mother if she tells anyone that they squeeze too close to her on the school bus seat. They interpret her fearful tears as success in gaining her attention and loyalty to them.

While on duty, you see this shy young girl and bookish, depressed-looking boy walk a little slower than the other kids. Behind them you see the larger, animated bully walking and talking with friends, in the midst of the rest of the chaos of students' happy-sounding voices. What actions, if any, should you take? Let me share a personal story that will help.

In sixth grade, I rode a school bus that had mostly high school kids on it. One day one of the senior boys decided to use me as a target for karate-chopping practice. He inflicted a blow against the front of my neck so well that I nearly passed out. My throat swelled so much I could hardly swallow. My voice went from low tenor to mezzo-soprano instantly. In spite of the pain I actually liked my new sound. My mother, on the other hand, became furious. The next morning I cringed with fear when Mom informed me that she would make sure an incident like that never happened to me again. A small woman, only five foot three and of moderate weight, my mother showed me that day how much she loved me and how to make sure that all the kids on that bus knew it.

When the bus arrived in front of our house, I got on as always and walked toward the back looking for an open seat. I found one and quickly shrank into it as my mother mounted the steps and stopped at the top, staring from face to face, showing each of the curious teenagers her anger. Then she did it. In a very stern voice she told everyone that I had suffered a needless injury and that if anything like that ever happened to me or any of the other kids on the bus again, whoever did it would answer to her. I think I actually saw fire come out of her mouth as she made what was in my mind a horrifying promise. She told them that every child on that bus deserved to be respected and not to live in fear of a simple-minded bully. Having made that statement, she looked again into the face of each student on the bus, then exited. That was one of the quietest bus rides in history. No one giggled or mumbled all the way to school. I was certain I would get even worse treatment for having told my mother. But instead, I received much better treatment from everyone, even the bully, for the rest of the school year.

Now, I am not suggesting that you jump on the bus every time you suspect a bully has hurt another child, but I am saying you must not shrink from your obligation as teacher, adult, and leader. Mom was right. Everyone deserves the respect of others rather than living in fear of them. I recently found a book of poems written by children about bullying, and the meaning in their youthful messages was clear. They feared and were intimidated by bullies. Their ability to function as children, students, and, I am sure, as the adult citizens they grew up to become, was impaired by having to wonder if they would suffer yet another indignity before the sun lowered beyond the horizon. You should always treat aggression as a choice the bullying child has made.

Cyber Bullying

Today bullying has moved into the digital arena. A bully can do such things as send e-mails with ugly rumors or lies using another person's e-mail address, resulting in misunderstandings, hurt feelings, and even physical harm. Blogs can be used to spread vicious rumors that can be read by anyone in the world, anywhere in the world. MySpace and Facebook pages can be constructed to taunt and harass other students. Using this media for such evil gives the modern-day cyber bully unbelievable potential for causing grief.

You should become aware of what your students are doing on the Internet because it may include cyber-bullying. Try periodic Internet searches on your students' names. By doing this you may also learn potentially useful information that will, at least, help you know them better.

You probably can't stop this type of deviant human behavior, but you will be able to understand its potential to reduce the learning that takes place in your classroom.

THE FEAR I know that one of the students in my school has used the Internet to send out evil lies about another student. I have heard the kids talking about it, but don't know what to do.

THE SOLUTION Since you may never find out who inflicted such pain because of the anonymity of the Internet, you cannot punish the perpetrator. You can, however, discuss the use of such deplorable tactics as those of a coward unable to face his or her opponent. You can also go to some websites to learn more about this. Here are a couple I have found: *www.antibullying.net* and stopbullyingnow .hrsa.gov. I am sure there are many more ways to stay educated on the evolving tactics used by bullies.

LET'S SUMMARIZE . . .

❶ The physical signs of victims of bullying become readily apparent.

❷ You must work harder to discover the victims of emotional bullying, but the help you can provide to them is no less needed.

❸ Bullies seem to operate more effectively at the elementary level than the secondary, but that may only appear to be the case; when they're older they have graduated to using psychological forms of inflicting fear on their victims.

❹ Aggression is a choice. Treat it as such.

CHAPTER 14

How Am I Supposed to Stop School Violence?

There is a hysteria that surrounds school violence. You can choose to believe the media-hyped stereotypes that have created another scenario like *War of the Worlds* and by doing so perpetuate a culture ravaged by fear, or you can find the truth. Look for facts and scientific evidence before falling for amped-up reports of isolated events appearing as trends. True, school violence is an important issue and it does occur; however, it should not be blown out of proportion, making it seem unconquerable, which it isn't. You do have the power to end your fear of school violence.

It has been said that a difficult issue can be changed one person at a time, and that the change begins with one person standing up against the problem. So how do you change this culture that brings violence into your classroom? Begin today.

Don't Believe the Hype

When I was still in the corporate world, I read about gang activity, the Columbine High School shootings, and other evidences of school violence erupting in our public schools. I felt what I thought was a healthy fear of all teens who lived in our world. I thought our society had lost its way by creating such a deviant human element. I knew it had to become progressively worse as these youths became adults. I wondered how our country would survive. I wondered if the possibility still existed for this society to produce honorable politicians who would become honorable leaders.

I failed to realize that advocacy groups use surveys to draw attention to their causes, and that no matter how grave they make it sound, if you dig deeper, you will find that the potential for disaster is less than reported most of the time. Remember, you should be wary of reports that something has doubled over a certain period of time, unless there are verified numbers to support this increase. For example, if I say the incidents of stabbings in America's high schools has doubled from 2002 to 2007, that sounds very alarming. However, if you look closer and find that while the number of incidents grew from 100 in 2002 to 200 in 2007, the student population has grown in that time period, this "alarming" statistic loses some of its fright.

Your Fear Is Natural

Alarming statistics aside, high school students can be imposing figures. My fear hit when I saw a group of football players working out with weights. Those guys pressed more weight over their heads than I could drag using a four-wheel-drive Jeep. I prayed for strength to handle my fear. I knew I needed to face a classroom full of renegade teens without flinching. You, too, must do this. Guess what? When you show them respect, they will return that respect and your fear will turn into love for them and your work.

You can't act as a referee, and the school has rules that tell you what to do if an actual fight occurs. So make sure you know those rules.

Help Students Find Their True Identities

Kids use masks to create their identity depending on how they feel that day. As they get older they begin to figure out their own identity, which will eventually rise to the surface. Your job of teaching includes recognizing these masks and continually trying to help the students find the real person behind the façade. The sooner your students understand who they are, the less likely they are to strike out in fear. As discussed by Carol Maxym and Leslie B. York in their book *Teens in Turmoil*, teenagers become especially good at wearing their myriad of masks, not the least of which includes those reflecting power and control.

The question of how to break up a fight becomes not how to physically separate the warring parties, but how to determine why they fight. This determination as to why a student fights relies heavily on his personal identity and the identity of the group with whom he socializes.

Take a page from the corporate world. Before I could succeed in making a business connection turn into a good business relationship, I had to learn as much as I could about the customer. Then I could determine whether my products could fill his needs and whether (and this is the important one) I could sustain the relationship over time. I knew that the value of repeat customers far outweighed the profitability of gaining new ones. Knowledge of the customer's focus and motives resulted in higher long-range profits for my company.

Once you know the inner rhythms of your students, you will understand how they continually try to integrate themselves into the picture they have of themselves without benefit of a concept of the future. Their minds whirl around in a paradox of feelings, dramatically swinging from invincibility to total fear of the world and themselves. Their only consistency is a word they often use today, a word that means the same thing it did when we used it as kids and teens. It's the one word they use to define what they want to be. Unlike words that change meaning with the blowing of the wind, whether they are standard English or concocted by the teenage brain, this one survives all the mood swings and fads of growing up. The word is "cool." They all want to be "cool."

Kids and Being "Cool"

Whatever you do, don't ask kids to define "cool." They will react with every feeling from disdain to incredulity to befuddlement, and will conceal these feelings with aloofness. You will feel a chill as you get that look that says, "Why are you asking me such a stupid question? Are you trying to trap me, or what?" The look is actually a stall tactic while they try to find their definition and then a way to explain it in terms that you, who is no longer young, will understand.

You really don't need to obtain an answer because you already know that to be cool is to be desirable to all other kids in their world, and to do so without effort. Obviously, you know this cannot happen in a real world, especially in a world filled with people wearing masks that depend on how they feel about themselves, which changes daily. The mature adult inside you knows each student and understands how they function in their world. They want to be different and the same concurrently. The result is that they become very predictable. But, what if their predictability involves violent behavior?

The Violent Ones

The many sources of childhood violent behavior make the predictability of its execution difficult. Watch for changes in mood. The choices of clothing can indicate these mood swings because the clothing represents the image or inner perspective of the child that day. Even in a school where the students wear uniforms, their hair care, fingernail polish, earrings, and choice of shoes and other accessories signal these changes. The sentences used in conversation that begin with "like," and the students' reaction to your directive with "whatever" (emphasis on "ever"), diminish or dismiss altogether the meaning of your comment. Don't think for one minute that they didn't hear you. They did, but they do not, and I emphasize *do not*, want you to know it, or they lose what they consider control over the situation and therefore over themselves.

Depression and the resulting rejection of the adult world because it doesn't understand them are symptoms of the most dangerous slippery slope for adolescents and teens. Sliding down this slope, greased by groups of kids or gangs, becomes easier and easier the closer they get to the actual mindset of the gang. Violence becomes the natural result, and especially violence against the establishment, or adult world, because of the perception that it not only doesn't understand, but imposes its will on the adolescents or teens, thereby taking away their control over themselves.

Be aware of your moral base. The wrongful action done yesterday remains the wrongful action done today. Just because wrongful acts increase in frequency doesn't make them okay. Don't let these wear you down, because allowing that to happen erodes your moral base, and that becomes your slippery slope.

Do you see the common thread running through all this? It's "they." These egocentric humans cannot allow intrusions into their world or they lose their perceived ability to act out their free will. They do not understand the true definition of freedom. For example, have you ever had one of your students react to one of your rules by telling you she knows you have violated her rights?

When your rules and discipline go so deep as to eliminate all feeling of control, the student must do something to stop it, and that "something" can result in violence. It can erupt as everything from senseless vandalism to mass murder. Make sure you watch for the signs. You cannot take the handling of violent actions lightly. Focus on finding the cause in order to stop violence and eradicate your fear.

THE FEAR I am a young, five foot two inch female. I teach high school and many of the boys and girls tower over me. When I walk down the hallway between classes to go to the restroom I find myself surrounded and constantly bumped by kids rushing to their next class while talking to each other, seemingly oblivious to my presence. It frightens me and I have yelled at them when they do it, but they usually don't even slow down.

THE SOLUTION I have a friend who recently retired from teaching and jokingly said she couldn't pee until a bell rang, but was trying to adapt. That comment actually made me realize how we become such creatures of habit, especially physically, that we become stuck in a rut we don't like but do nothing about. I believe it was Thoreau who said "the mass of men lead lives of quiet desperation." Even when what we do contains an element of fear, we continue.

Most schools have strict instructions to teachers to not leave the classroom unattended, and to maintain a presence in the halls so the students will behave themselves while changing classes. These result in our fighting the crowd to relieve ourselves. Due to my advanced years I feel I can take the risk of upsetting some of the older teachers who suffer from the malady I call S.B.S., or "shrinking bladder syndrome" (everything causing physical inconvenience is called a syndrome these days), by stating that you can actually train your bladder to allow you to relieve it at preplanned times. You must understand that this training involves appropriate diet and timing of the consumption of certain liquids. I know what works for me, but you will have to experiment with your own diet.

The other factor involves students' recognizing you in their midst. Appropriate dress will assist in this. You must dress like the professional you are. Your demeanor, which is not that of a friend interested in their life but of an adult to whom they owe respect, will also help. Always remember that you can and should act friendly toward your students, but you cannot actually befriend them.

Finally, stand in the doorway to your classroom to welcome your students as they arrive. Doing this tells them you not only recognize them as valuable human beings, but that they are important to you.

LET'S SUMMARIZE . . .

❶ The world now reels with increased violence and violent kids.

❷ The media influences your perception of this violence.

❸ The kids identify their feelings by the way they dress, their hygienic practices, and their friends. Pay attention to these flags.

❹ Not all kids are violent, and most will never become violent, but those who are need careful attention.

❺ The common thread within the personality of all children, regardless of age, is egocentricity.

CHAPTER 15

Why Do My Students Keep Getting Distracted?

Aren't there any two kids that are alike anymore? Were there ever two alike? If you teach today you have asked yourself questions like that.

We base our teachings and their success on modern practices of educational diversity. But before these practices were put into place, how did we get a leader like Abraham Lincoln, or a corporate legend like Jack Welch (former chairman of General Electric), or a marketing wizard like Sam Walton (founder of Wal-Mart), or an economic intellectual giant like Alan Greenspan (former chairman of the Federal Reserve and author of *The Age of Turbulence*)? How could our schools have produced these very different individuals? Easy, you say, because they were geniuses. Maybe, or maybe the simpler ways of teaching back then worked in times more simple than today.

In today's driven society, you and your students may feel lost or useless if you are not multitasking. Your students don't know any other way, and they really think boredom will kill them. They must fill every waking moment with multiple inputs to bombard their minds. However, if they can listen to the latest chart-topper, eat a meal, and play some killer video game all at the same time, why do they find it so difficult, if not impossible, to focus on reading *The Village Blacksmith*, then write about a person in today's world who performs analogous work in their town, and follow it up by working on a linear equation, showing all the steps toward solution?

You need to get them to focus by making your classroom a diverse learning environment.

Teaching to Various Intellectual Levels

Abraham Lincoln attended a one-room schoolhouse. What could be more diverse than students in grade levels from first to twelfth all in one room with the same teacher? But that was another time and, although the room was filled with diversity, the teacher and the lessons were not. Even though the school buildings grew and changed their look, there remained a dreaded consistency of content to be choked down, memorized, and regurgitated back as knowledge.

Humans do have a tendency to rely on monotonous, mind-numbing, cookie-cutter regularity. Most of us shrink away from change. We hope that we have misunderstood our senses, and that the appearance of change really isn't real. However, the truth is that once we understand a change that has occurred, it will improve our lives. So, why should we find it so disturbing and scary?

Keep on Your Toes to Keep Your Students Interested

Even after more than forty years as a successful stand-up comedian, Red Skelton still became so nervous that he threw up before a performance. I hope you don't do that, especially because you will be performing for several hours, and your brain needs that fuel for creativity and stamina.

Don't worry, your love for the teaching profession will help you to maintain a high level of performance throughout many years, and your students will benefit because of it. After all, what other profession requires you to:

- Achieve a high level of continuous education
- Have a working knowledge of psychology
- Possess the diplomatic skills of a U.S. Secretary of State
- Be able to hold an audience for as long as six hours
- Exercise effective discipline without corporal forms of punishment
- Start the day before dawn and end long after the sun has set
- Provide educational guidance to young minds busy with other activities
- Lend a shoulder when needed
- Make certain to give just the right amount of praise

All of this is done in the hope that you will spark a fire in the mind of a future Ernest Hemingway or John F. Kennedy.

If you think about all the ways people spend time today compared to the days of Lincoln or Hemingway, the need for teaching to diverse learning styles becomes obvious. Will that remove your fear of diversity? No, it won't, but putting the diverse needs of today's kids into perspective should help to prepare you.

Try to learn how to do something you have never done before, such as speak another language, or perhaps learn how to sign.

Spend the first precious days at the beginning of the school year learning about your new students. Read up on their learning histories. Talk to previous teachers. Test your new students in various ways. No one should fault you for doing this valuable research. So what if you wind up with several different levels of assignments? The students will feel special and learn at their own pace, and you will stay on top of how they are progressing so you can do what you are meant to do.

Issues with Diversity

As mentioned, people from around the world once referred to the United States as a "melting pot" of humanity. You cannot, and should not, ignore that as our heritage. That expression meant that people from all around the world emigrated from their countries to live in the United States, and they built it as a nation. Today we still have a large population of immigrants.

I don't need to tell you that many of the immigrants' countries of origin have their own languages. You must also realize that they have their own cultures as well. The culture shock that immigrants suffer makes learning a new language even more difficult. Please don't make the mistake of thinking this is not important. I know of its importance firsthand.

Several years ago I accepted a position in the company for which I worked that required moving to France for one or two years. Even though my wife and I took a course in conversational French, we experienced quite the culture shock upon arriving in France. France isn't a third-world country, and it has all the same things the United States does, such as shopping centers, supermarkets, highways, corporate businesses, and the like. However, the small things are what provided the real shock.

The country's emphasis on cooking, having stylish clothes and using expensive perfumes, and the practice of bringing pets everywhere definitely threw us off. The fact that the previous tenants of all the apartments we looked into renting took the major appliances with them in their move was an inconvenient surprise.

Another came when we learned that parents often put their children to bed and then went out to a restaurant alone for dinner. Can you imagine?

My wife and I longed for someone to greet us in English; for a waiter who wouldn't act extremely put out by the mere existence of our children with us as we all enjoyed a meal; and to be able to walk down a street and enjoy the fresh air while not worrying about watching our every step for dog poo.

Does this make us American snobs? Of course not. Do all immigrants want to work menial jobs and live in harsh conditions? Of course not. Do you need to fear diversity in your classroom? Of course not. However, you must be prepared to learn the customs of your new students and understand their immigrant culture in order to reduce your fear.

Kids from the "Other Side of the Tracks"

The "other side of the tracks" is an old expression simply meaning anyone different from and less affluent than you. Kids judge each other superficially. It takes many years of educating and maturity before humans can assess others by who they are and not who they look like. You must know this and learn the different social classes who make up the population of your school and the communities in which they live. You will not get to them until you understand them.

At the risk of oversimplification of developing an understanding of your students, you should test their diversities in as many ways as possible. Some of those ways include:

- If you teach students in their earliest formative years, have them draw things like their family, their home, or their car.

- Once your students have learned to write, have them write letters to a friend about a recent experience, a family outing, or their list of gifts they want for their birthday.
- Form your students into groups so that students from different cultures must work together to complete a project.
- Create an informal debate about a current issue of national importance, and select teams to work together on the research for the debate. Allow them to pick team member assignments such as who gives the first speech and who writes their notes during the debate.

You choose the ways your students must interact in your classroom. Pay close attention to those interactions and the results while remaining equally interested in each student.

THE FEAR Whenever I try to get my students to work with students outside of their clique, they do the assignment without any enthusiasm or imagination and return to their own group of friends as soon as they have any opportunity. I have come up with great group assignments, and have tried several different forms of random selection to form the groups. How can I get them to understand the value of the diversity within the class?

THE SOLUTION Your students are simply doing what comes naturally, resisting change. As long as they perceive the groups in your classroom as your groups, they will not change and interact the way you want. There are games you can play that will demonstrate to them the need to interact with students they perceive as different from themselves. One such game involves asking questions about their likes and dislikes and having them form groups based on their answers. This results in friends in friends' groups. Next you ask questions that can best be solved by people who don't necessarily think alike. You require them to regroup into "their" groups which just happen to be groups that consist of students who have different likes, dislikes, levels of knowledge on a subject, and on and on. Now they have formed the groups and so the groups belong to them. Obviously, you need to know your students to make this work, but using this technique you will dramatically increase their enthusiasm and thus learning.

LET'S SUMMARIZE . . .

❶ There are no two groups of kids that are alike now, and there never were.

❷ Although we can group kids by intellectual capabilities, each one within each group has his or her own capabilities. Take the time to discover them.

❸ Today's language and ethnic differences need attention, but this is not new to America.

❹ Within your group you will find diversity based on geographic location of each of their homes, and that location depends on factors such as income level, race, and many more. Learn as much as you can about the demographics of the community.

CHAPTER 16

What If *They* Are Scared?

Recently I watched a movie in which a disgruntled National Security Agency employee used the digital world in his attempt to prove his point of our vulnerability to a terrorist cyber attack. He found the centralized controls for our sources of electrical power, water supply, and finances, and used this information to nearly take control of the United States.

In recent years I have used computerized scheduling for lesson planning; maintained computerized financial records for my company, as well as records of my personal investments; and researched online databases of government records. Because of that background I bought into the movie's concept (except for the sensationalized parts where the hero performs impossible physical feats, of course). Therefore, it's easy to understand why the teens I teach would not only buy into such a heinous concept but allow a latent fear of cyber terrorism to disturb them.

Students' Access to Frightening Information

According to an article in the *Washington Post*, there are actually manuals available on the web for Supervisory Control and Data Acquisition (SCADA), which is used to control the digital systems for dams, electrical power grids, water treatment plants, and sewage treatment facilities as well as oil and gas utilities. The Worldwide Incidents Tracking System (available on the web at *http://wits.nctc.gov*) indicates that seventeen terrorist incidents occurred in the United States from February 2, 2004, to September 11, 2006. With a minimal amount of time and reference knowledge you can use the web to learn about terrorist attacks using anthrax or dirty bombs, or threats of such attacks. You can discover that al-Qaeda networks have chemical warfare capability. If you can easily get this information, you have to believe your students can get it, and more. The question is, do they?

In the halls of my school, more is said about global warming than anything to do with the kinds of potential terror just mentioned. Does that mean no fear of those types of terror permeates our schools? You will have to be the judge of your own school environment. The reason for academic emphasis on global warming versus terror is the scientific curiosity connected with global warming, and the fear we all have of unnecessarily alarming our students about the threat of terror. We fear telling them about something so potentially devastating because their immature minds can't handle it. Well, here's a revelation. They know about real terror and they fear it just as we do. All of them have televisions, and adults at home who talk about it.

Students' Reactions to Frightening Information

You already know that your students, no matter their age, bring ideas and ideals from their home into your classroom. However, the ability to stand back and assess a situation, analyze it, draw conclusions, and understand consequences escapes most of them. Therefore, the sources of their fears are movies, television, parents, bullies, peers, and you. It is your job to alleviate those fears by dismissing any that are unsubstantiated and assuring them of their safety in the case of those that are actual threats.

Believe it or not, the *Harry Potter* series, with its depth of fantasy-filled imagination, is a source of fear among young adolescents. Hogwarts Castle isn't exactly the most inviting place in the world, and within the series of Rowling's books the fictional school is constantly under attack from outside forces. Understanding these fears allows you to direct their influences by helping the student understand whether their fears are real or not. You can help them understand that the unbelievable things happening in Hogwarts Castle are just as much fantasy as the plight of the acorn-chasing squirrel in *Ice Age*. You also can alleviate your students' fears of an attack on your school by giving them a thorough and compassionate explanation of the emergency plans put in place. It will teach them the importance of dealing with such a situation as safely as possible.

> Always keep in mind that you may have students who have a parent or parents who are in the military and fighting overseas, or who have lost a parent in combat, or who have a crime-fighting parent who may or may not have fallen in action. They will have fears the others don't.

What about When We Were Kids?

Sure, we had our fantasy with *The Wizard of Oz*, *Alice in Wonderland*, and *Labyrinth*, but we weren't bombarded at the same time by a world filled with identity theft, anthrax, children committing mass murder, and dirty-bomb threats. We had role models who played sports using their God-given talents, not relying on performance-enhancing drugs. Most of us had a home that gave us a soft place to land. It may not have been easier growing up when we did, but it was most likely a lot simpler than the time now, when your students are coming of age. You need to remember that they are going through the necessary stages of adolescent development with some unnecessary side issues.

The Importance of Drills

When a recent lockdown drill was over, I told my students I was very pleased with their actions. I added that the students who sat on the floor with their heads below the tabletops as instructed were still alive, and that made me very happy. That room was filled with high school juniors and seniors, and getting them to comply with one of our "stupid" administrator's "stupid" drills is normally very difficult, especially when they see no imminent danger. At that age they resist any action toward group conformity. However, I used it as an opportunity to teach. After the drill I talked to them about the connection of school violence and world terror organizations.

I told them about how the destruction of a strong country such as the United States could best be achieved by destroying education systems that teach democracy and basic human rights. I allowed plenty of time for their responses, giving them an opportunity to verbalize their understanding and fear of terror. Does spending this time away from my academic teaching result in an adjustment to my lessons planned for that day? Yes, it does. Is it worth it? It most certainly is.

We cannot expect to teach our students how to function in our world while being completely isolated from that world. Do I risk increasing their fears by focusing attention on the terror that exists in our world? Yes, but doing so helps them place the emphasis on their important fears and away from the unfounded fears created by a fantasy world. Somewhere during my childhood a teacher told me I should only worry about things I can do something about, and to discard worrying about those things over which I have no control.

So What Do They Fear?

Your class is most likely made up of students from all types of religious backgrounds. You probably have Christians, Catholics, Protestants, Muslims, Jews, Hindus, Buddhists, and non-faith-based children. Also, your students will come from a variety of different kinds of homes, including two-parent homes, those with a stepparent, single-parent homes, and those presided over by a legal guardian. No matter their religious, societal, or family background, they have a basic belief system through which they filter all your input, interpreting it to suit their needs.

I never cease to be amazed at some of the comments I get when discussing "We Wear a Mask" by Paul Laurence Dunbar. In his poem, this black poet expresses how we all allow the world to understand us. After giving it some thought nearly 100 percent of my students agree that they, too, wear masks. Even though still in the tender years of their development, they recognize that they display their personalities differently for different people. They may not really understand why they do this, but do recognize doing it.

Once they reach puberty, their greatest fear is non-acceptance by their peers. In some this fear is so great as to rule out all others. In others, while this fear is their greatest, they also have fear of failing in school, fear of disappointing their family, fear of not succeeding in a sport, and last, fear that the terrorism in the world may interfere with their lives. A child's world is focused on friendships and school, so they fear disruption of those elements of their lives. Knowing this will allow you to find ways to introduce the adult understanding of world terrorism into their world without disturbing their ability to focus on their academic studies. For example, geometry and physics classes offer the opportunity to discuss the use of satellites for locating suspicious operations in defense of our country. Mathematics offers the opportunity to explain crime analysis that may or may not be terror related. Language arts offer ways to aid in understanding ethnic differences and learn how misunderstandings between nations occur. Web design offers the opportunity to explain cyber crime.

You must look at the bigger picture to understand the smaller one. In other words, you need to stay on top of local, national, and world news so you can weave our world into your classroom. You teach because you like learning, so consider yourself a student of the world. Listen to several news sources or read more than one written news account to broaden your understanding. Stay educated about what's happening in the world so you can in turn educate your students and ease their fears as well as your own.

THE FEAR I know they tune me out when I talk about the necessity of finding alternative energy sources or walking or riding bicycles instead of driving. How can I get my point across when they lack any desire to listen or understand? It's like they don't even hear me.

THE SOLUTION I can't offer any one fail-safe solution because every person is different and every classroom has its own dynamics. What I can offer is this: *they do hear you.* However, they probably do not want to seem like they hear you in order to fit in with their friends.

You must continue in your efforts, but you must make sure you keep their world in mind. If you are able to relate to them on the same level and make listening the "cool" thing to do, your students will start acting like they care about what you are saying. And once a few start acting that way, they will all catch on.

LET'S SUMMARIZE . . .

❶ The kids understand and make more sense out of digital forms of cyber terrorism than the physical forms represented by such organizations as al-Qaeda.

❷ The kids fear global warming more than global terrorism because of the scientific curiosity of academia.

❸ Don't forget that you may have students who belong to people of all faiths and political persuasions, and that you must remain sensitive to those important influences on their lives.

❹ Fear of losing friendships takes first place in the child's world. You must realize that fact in order to understand that your fear of terrorism will not seem all that important to them.

❺ You may have some kids who have lost a parent due to wars or to fighting crimes. You must be sensitive to their fears.

❻ You have a big job in gaining and maintaining knowledge of local, national, and global news, but you must do this to work those important events into your teaching.

PART III

Parental Fears

They have a big influence on how your

students act

_____

_____

_____

CHAPTER 17

Do My Students' Home Lives Come to School?

One day during your class you suddenly need to go to the restroom. The kids are diligently working on an assignment so you excuse yourself. You stop in the classroom next door and tell the teacher where you're going and ask her to keep an eye on your kids for a few minutes. You know you shouldn't leave your classroom, but sometimes nature has other plans.

Upon your return you see three boys quickly seating themselves. You call all three up front and ask them what they were doing and remind them, in your sternest voice, that they could not have had a valid reason for getting out of their seats. Out of the corner of your eye you notice that your favorite pot with its beautifully blooming African violets is missing. You stop talking to the boys long enough to scan the room for it and you see the remains of it on the floor, the pot broken in pieces, potting soil scattered, and the plant already beginning to wilt as it lies near one of the shards of pottery.

You temper escalates, but you quickly squelch it. Pointing to the wounded plant, you ask the boys what happened. At first they say nothing, but under your threat to keep all three after school, one begins providing an explanation in a very suspect manner.

The others say nothing, but steal furtive glances at each other. When the master storyteller finishes his tale, placing the blame on the other two, you tell them how much you loved that plant and that they must clean up the mess immediately. You give them a special disciplinary writing assignment for that evening, and then get on with class.

Because they "fessed up" they got a lighter punishment and avoided having to explain to their parents why they had to stay after school. You feel they got your message of how much you valued the plant and quickly restored order to your classroom. What you didn't know was that the one who placed blame on the other two had actually grabbed the potted plant from its perch on the windowsill and thrown it at one of the boys. In turn, the two got out of their seats to clean up the mess. The thrower stood and chastised them, calling them wimps. That's when you returned and they all tried to quickly return to their seats. The resultant backlash you received from the innocent boys' parents shocked and dismayed you. What should you have done?

Rather than acting out of fear of losing control of your classroom, or perhaps even fear of the boys, you should have taken more time to determine guilt. Your fear of losing control of your classroom by taking too much time in handling the situation is unfounded and will ultimately hurt your classroom management. I will be the first to support not giving an offender too much attention, because that is exactly what he is looking for. The longer he can make the disturbance last the less time you have to teach, and the more his ego is stroked.

He also beat your interrogation. As the aggressor, he knows what he says will go, and the other two would say nothing due to his bullying. If he said nothing, the others would say nothing and that would have caused uncertainty in your mind and an increased punishment. By volunteering his lie, he has eliminated your uncertainty, knowing that this action would reduce the punishment. So, he wins.

He knew your fear of a lengthy classroom disturbance and used it skillfully. He learned this either from previous disturbances in your classroom or from home. If he learned it from your previous actions, you must work on your discipline. If he learned it at home, you need to learn more about him.

This type of behavior shows that he wants control and attention, and knows that he can gain it through manipulation and intimidation. If this is the case, it's not happening solely in your classroom, and other teachers will be able to verify this for you. You need to ask them, and then talk to the school counselors and his parents.

Talking to his parents will give you a handle on what is happening in the home. The majority of the time, a troublesome student has an unstable home life. Whatever the issues are at home, they have caused him to lose his ability to trust others. He has learned that lying is an effective way to get what he wants. His home life has trained him in the art of manipulation, since he uses such tactics to get attention from his parents. He absolutely will bring this skill to school, using it to bully other students, and you, because doing so fulfills his need for attention.

Dealing with Their Baggage

You are the only adult in the room. Therefore, you are the only one who realizes that actions always have consequences. You may never know how a child's parents handle household problems or separation and divorce. Getting that close to the situation is not advisable. You are not a psychiatrist or a marriage counselor. However, you most likely have enough students in your classroom dealing with not-so-good situations at home that you need to be prepared. My goal here is not to delve too deeply into the effect of marital issues on the children in this country, because I am not qualified in either marriage counseling or social work, but to make you aware that you must get to know enough about your students to reduce your fears and theirs.

Children drag all their problems with them everywhere in the hope that someone they encounter during their day will solve them. They do not know why they are inept at solving their problems, nor do they understand why they have so many of them. They just have them. You all have children around you every day. Use this as your laboratory for continuing your education in dealing with their problems. Pay close attention to how they react not only to you but to each other.

My wife will be the first to tell you I didn't pay close enough attention to our own children. I relied on her good judgment and advice rather than take time from my busy business schedule to learn on my own. Shame on me. Now that I focus on teaching and am surrounded by kids all day, I have become dedicated to learning as much as possible from every source available. My students, my principal, and my students' parents should accept no less.

Paying attention to all their interactions says volumes. You will see the bullies, the cliques, the kids from unhappy or broken families, and the kids who come from happy, loving families. You then can build on this information through discussions with other teachers, guidance counselors, administrators, and also the parents of the kids struggling with their studies or self-worth.

What about the Children?

Never forget they are children. The rules that apply to your conduct do not apply to them. No matter whether they are five years old or fifteen, they cannot bear the burdens of their own personal crises and hear about your problems as well. You need to be mindful not to discuss your own outside issues with them as if the students were your peers. You are the teacher and they are the students. If they need to express the anger and hurt of a horrible personal life, it's not appreciated, but it's understandable. You, on the other hand, cannot do the same. Save it for your friends.

The students too will take their problems to their friends. Students will go to school and share things with classmates they feel close to. As children begin developing friendships, they also begin to feel that those friends can help resolve their problems simply because they are peers and understand each other.

What Happens When the Baggage Is Too Much?

When the smelly, dirty boy comes into your classroom, collapses into a desk and falls asleep, and the girl who sits next to him whacks him with a textbook, telling him in language littered with f*** to get away from her, your challenge is to calm her down and figure out what to do with the boy. He more than likely smells because his filthy home has no hot water, because the water or gas bill wasn't paid.

The girl would not have reacted this way if she too was dirty. So, you walk to where she is seated and quietly and calmly ask her if she would like to trade places with the boy. Tell her that we all come from different backgrounds and lifestyles and she should consider that before making any more outbursts.

Then turn to the boy and, if he is still asleep, wake him with a gentle nudge and a calm voice. Ask him if he feels okay or if he would like to go see the school nurse. If he says that he would, send him there and be assured the nurse will ask appropriate hygiene questions. If he doesn't want the nurse, then calmly remind him he is in class and he needs to pay attention. Then, continue with class, but follow up by contacting the school counselor and his family to learn why he came to school as he did.

Your job involves knowing as much as you can about your students so you can, hopefully, get them to learn something, and so that your knowledge of their personal circumstances allows you to remain calm and objective around them. Yours may be the only voice of compassion or love some of your students ever hear. So hear it they must. Don't deprive them of what little love you can offer or heap more problems on them by venting your own.

THE FEAR I teach English to middle school children. After showing my eighth graders the movie, *E.T. The Extra Terrestrial,* I asked them to write an essay commenting on whether or not they thought it had a deeper message than just the fantasy they saw on the screen. One of them wrote a terribly scathing commentary using word selections and phrasing reflecting tremendous anger that frightened me. Should I have confronted him to discuss this anger?

THE SOLUTION Most adolescents enjoy that movie as pure fantasy. Some may be frightened by the thought of an alien, but in that age group they enjoy it when they realize there is no danger connected with it. Anger is a strange response and bears looking into, but not by direct confrontation. Grade the paper based on your normal English essay requirements and add a note thanking him for expressing his point of view. Then follow up by expressing your concerns to the school counselor.

LET'S SUMMARIZE . . .

❶ One guarantee about kids that you can count on is they will bring whatever problems they have at home into your classroom.

❷ If kids learn that they can get their way at home by manipulating their family, they will expect to do the same in school.

❸ You must learn as much about child and family relationships as possible to enhance your ability to create a great learning environment in your classroom.

❹ Everyone has fears encroaching on his or her life. Learning about their source reduces them significantly.

CHAPTER 18

Why Do My Students' Parents Scare Me?

The helicopters are hovering. The term "helicopter parent" surfaced in recent years in reference to the ever-present, ever-fearful parent. Some college guidance counselors refer to such parents as "Black Hawks" due to their increased intrusions, and even reference the near-panic mode of some parents by referring to them as "Kamikazes." All of these descriptions identify the modern-day phenomenon of parents who not only can't let go, but go well beyond the purview of concerned parents, involving themselves so deeply into their children's lives that they create a disruptive influence in your classrooms.

Far from the apathetic parent (discussed in Chapter 19), many of these parents are "in your face." You undoubtedly have encountered the parents concerned about their child's progress in your class. You welcomed these parents. At least they were concerned enough to come in and visit with you to discuss reasons for their child's issues. But, the hovering, overprotective intrusion of a parent who can't tell the difference between genuine concern and keeping the reins so tight they choke the life out of their children, and cause your stress level to skyrocket, creates in you a fear of complex proportions.

Many psychologists reason that these hovering "friends of their children" became so addicted to helping their child because they were baby boomers who experienced the turmoil of the 1960s, when everyone seemed confused. Additionally, many feel they work hard to provide a good education for their children and that because the economic costs are so high, they have a "right" to make sure they get their money's worth. These parents often have little faith in the teaching abilities of the American school systems because they see the United States falling behind other countries. Their own life-style, created by working in our fast-paced, highly stressed business world with its focus on profits and the concomitant lack of worker job security, often causes them to treat their personal lives, and the lives of their children, with that same level of assertiveness.

These modern-day parental control freaks have become such a problem at the college level that some colleges have set up protective units. These units consist of students whom they train to divert the unwanted parent from orientation and other such meetings.

How to Handle the Helicopters

The reasons for this parental aggressiveness are many, and far too complicated to deal with in this book, ranging from the teacher/parent who always knows better ways to teach than you do to the aggressive professional or executive accustomed to using intimidation to succeed. It is you, however, who must find ways to deal with them without making them even more intrusive, while still leaving time to teach all the students in your classroom. In order to do this you need the proper equipment.

An Example from the Business World

I have had the opportunity through my business career to deal with adults of all shapes and sizes and intellectual capacities.

Some of them also had phobias and other psychological flaws that led them to make strange decisions and to have difficulty relating to others. Yet many such individuals succeeded in amassing great wealth and then using it to "get their way" and intimidate their subordinates, as well as to negotiate business deals slanted extremely well in their favor. I would like to share with you one such experience.

I had recently accepted a new executive position. Shortly after settling into my new position I discovered I had to do business with the most feared businessman ever encountered by anyone in this company. Did they believe I could handle this so-called beast when they hired me, or did they "sandbag" me hoping I would sink under this man's enormous pressure? Either way is moot at this point. I heard so many rumors about this guy that when the day came and my phone rang, and my assistant announced his name, I felt my innards turn to mush. He did not disappoint his reputation. Something had occurred that angered him, and I received the brunt of his wrath. So, what did I do?

I listened without comment while he vented, and took careful notes of his points so I could address each one in the order in which he had spewed them at me. Once he stopped I allowed a brief pause before responding, and then began my responses in the order as written in my notes. I knew he wouldn't like all of my answers, but I also knew giving him truthful and accurate information was the way to go. Some of my responses required follow-up on my part, so I gave him exact dates when I would get back to him. He reluctantly accepted my responses, but not without threatening some serious repercussions including getting me fired if I didn't follow through. I couldn't wait to actually meet him.

I followed through as promised and he softened enough for a small degree of cordiality. The Christmas holidays were coming soon, so I took the opportunity to tell him of a special practice of giving that we instituted when I had my own business. He laughed a laugh of approval and added a brief comment about how he and his wife no longer gave each other gifts and instead used the money to develop a special foundation to help feed the homeless.

About a month later I went to his office to deal face to face with a very serious business problem. People in my office sent me off with comments of sympathy, fear, and prayers for me to survive. That, of course, magnified my fear level, but I also had learned something about this "bear," and I knew that knowledge would make everything work.

Soon I found myself sitting in his office while this hulk of a man yelled at someone on the phone. I took the moment before my confrontation with him to look around his office. What I saw reinforced my feeling of security in dealing with him. He had pictures of his wife and his children and grandchildren on his desk. On his wall were plaques commending him for his overall support of the community, and specifically for the poor. This was not a bad guy.

While he hung up the phone and yelled at an assistant to get something from his desk, I waited quietly. When the young girl quickly arrived in his office, he handed her some paper and barked orders at her. She almost physically shrank away from his desk, turned, and disappeared from the room, closing the door behind her. He turned his attention to me.

It was my turn.

I took the initiative by telling him that I knew something about him that he had successfully concealed from everyone in my company. He said nothing, but I had his attention. I told him not to waste his venomous attacking style on me, because it wouldn't work. I told him that underneath his blustery exterior there beat the heart of a kind, loving man. Then I waited for his response.

He stared at me with a look that would surely have melted the resolve of the most fearless lion. Finally he smiled before saying, "What makes you think that?"

At that moment I knew I was right. His smile told me he had focused on the last thought in my comment, about him being a kind, loving man. I told him that any man who so obviously loves his family and the less advantaged of God's people, who in fact loves them enough to give up some of his blessings for them, is simply a good person. Our conversation immediately became friendly as he told me of his angel business. (An angel business is similar to private funding of small businesses in need of financing. The difference between this type of business funding and normal financial funding of businesses is that the funding person neither expects nor requires anything in return, and there are no tax benefits involved.)

Our meeting ended after I gave him the bad news I had come to deliver. He accepted it with only a minor complaint, and he and his wife took me out to lunch. That was more than seven years ago, and we still remain friends to this day. Even though I am no longer in business, I know if I need something I can pick up the telephone, call him, and get it.

How It Relates to the Teaching World

Taking steps similar to those I took with that businessman will result in the vast majority of your meetings with hovering parents going well, and your fear diminishing or disappearing altogether. It's also important to keep in mind that it is very difficult to continue venting anger at someone who has apologized. That means you must be sure you apologize for any misunderstanding that may have occurred. It doesn't matter whether you have actually done anything that's wrong or deserving of their anger. You should keep the welfare of the child in mind. Sure, you won't cure "helicoptering," but you may reduce its degree of interference in your classroom by understanding it.

When dealing with this difficult client (parent) use the same approach as taken with my client as follows:

1. Listen to the other employees' (counselors or other teachers) comments.
2. Take the action of contacting the (parent) client.
3. Listen to the clients' (parents') problems.
4. Deal with the problems in the same order (using the parent's order of complaints or issues keeps the discussion in their frame of reference and lets them know you have listened carefully).
5. Remain calm enough to apply logic into the situation.
6. Make sure you know where the client (parent) is coming from before you respond.

I told you that story to tell you this: Someone once said that 90 percent of what we fear never happens. That doesn't mean you expect to succeed in every parental meeting. It does, however, mean that if you prepare yourself properly, your fear should and will diminish greatly and you will succeed more often than not.

Helen Johnson, a consultant on parental relations for some of America's top universities, has authored a book titled *Don't Tell Me What To Do, Just Send Money*, in which she explains that while some parents think they're just doing what is right for their children, they're actually doing exactly what's wrong for them. Their hovering parenting sends the message that their children can't do anything right or on their own.

THE FEAR I have a mother who e-mails complaints and offers her solutions every time her child fails to get an A on an assignment or test. Her daughter whines to me about the difficulty of every assignment and, if it contains several steps, complains and asks for clarification of each. Between the two of them, I need something to calm my nerves. The student nearly always gets an A, but never a 100 percent, and so her mother remains unhappy with me.

THE SOLUTION Respond quickly to the mother. First apologize for any misunderstanding, and then give her detailed explanations. Gently tell the student that a big part of the assignment is testing her ability to understand and follow written instructions. If the mother persists, call for a meeting with both her and her daughter. If the mother agrees, gently explain to her that a part of the assignment is the student following written instructions on her own. You should also add that making mistakes is one of life's best teachers as long as one pays attention to understanding the mistake and not making it again.

LET'S SUMMARIZE . . .

❶ Set up a meeting quickly when parents call with a complaint; be flexible while also showing a preference for meetings before classes start.

❷ Gather documentation of assignments and grades.

❸ Make certain you know and understand any Individualized Education Program (IEP) requirements for the student.

❹ Talk to other teachers and guidance counselors about the student.

❺ If at all possible, pick a meeting room where you won't be disturbed, and get there early.

❻ Dress professionally; welcome the parents with a friendly handshake; allow them to sit first; and use your teacher's power of observation to determine their attitude.

❼ Ask how you can help; take careful notes as they speak; resist temptations to interrupt to defend yourself if they are attacking you personally.

❽ Pause to gather your thoughts, then address each of their points in the same order they gave them.

❾ Remember that this meeting is not a time to teach, but to negotiate and even apologize, because the welfare of the child is at stake.

CHAPTER 19

How Do I Handle an Apathetic Parent?

Now you see them and now you don't. We dealt with aggressive parents in the previous chapter, but apathetic parents are just as troublesome, especially with their prevalence in our modern society. How many times have you read about people voting down a school levy? Reasons proffered by voters include reluctance to give more money when there's poor school administration, governmental misuse of funds, and corruption at the local level. However, the real reasons are likely to include these: parents-turned-voters are just too busy to care; they think teachers educate their kids, so clearly they're not doing their jobs well enough; or they simply like their lifestyle too much to put up with higher taxes.

More difficult forms of apathy or apparent lack of concern stem from an inferiority complex due to lack of parental education; language or cultural differences; or issues involving drug or alcohol abuse. You do not want to jump to the conclusion that a parent is apathetic without taking steps to make sure that is in fact the case. Just because a parent doesn't call for a meeting when a student has a failing grade in your class doesn't mean the parent doesn't care. Communication may seem to flow in only one direction, and you don't know for certain if anyone reads your messages, so you also have no way of knowing if the parent said anything to her child about your concern.

In order to make sure your message gets across, you must be "real." You must be the role model your student may need. Remind yourself that he needs you, even when it feels like he is sucking the life out of you by demanding your attention with personal issues and seemingly meaningless questions. His non-responsive parents may not only fail to respond to you, but, more important, they may not respond to their child either. So, always do the following:

- Have high, unchanging standards
- Let students know their actions always have consequences
- Let them know you have feelings
- Love them

Your students are your responsibility, even if their parents have decided to give up on their parental responsibilities.

Communication Is Key

Communicate with your students' parents or guardians often. The more you let them know, the less they will question what goes on in your classroom. But won't doing this make it hard to know whether a parent is apathetic or well informed? Actually, it's the contrary. Let me explain by a couple of examples.

Example #1: An Apathetic Parent

A student came to me one day and complained that he had received a zero for an assignment. His football coach told him he was ineligible due to failing a couple of classes, so he checked his Schoolone account (our school's online grade reporting system). I explained to him that the assignment involved classroom partici-pation, and he was absent that day. He wanted to make it up, but since it involved a group activity, I told him he couldn't because a classroom group assignment in my general business class equaled a day missed at work. Of course he declared that rule unfair. I reminded him that a responsible employee would not miss work without calling in to let the employer know he could not make it to work and why. I gave him a moment to think about that and asked him, "How long do you think you would have a job if you failed to show up for work?" Before he could say anything, I added that I would have fired him for an unexcused absence if he had worked for me when I ran my business. He thought about that for a moment before informing me that his mother missed work all the time and didn't call in, and she had worked for the same firm for thirty years.

That is when I said something in the hope of getting his attention. I told him she wasn't setting a very good example for him and that I wanted him to tell her I said that. I never heard from her.

This wasn't the first time I did something in an attempt to get his parents' attention. I have had this student, now a junior, since his freshman year, and in that time have sent e-mails and letters and left phone messages for his parents. I have yet to receive a call from them, let alone meet them. Their son is failing miserably. They pay a lot of tuition to send him to our school, and yet, they don't care enough to even get mad and call me, never mind show up for parent-teacher conferences. Should I give up? The answer is a resounding No. He will probably never graduate from our high school, but I remain hopeful he will remember the lessons of high standards, consequences for his actions, and my love for teaching and for him.

Example #2: A Well-Informed Parent

I originally thought this was a case of parental apathy, but it turned out to be something very different. It occurred with a student in my English class who sporadically completed her assignments. I always require my students to turn in their completed work on the due date and explain that I will deduct 10 percent from their grade for each day the assignment is late. Obviously, if they turn it in ten or more days late, they get a zero no matter how well they have accomplished it. This particular student could understand the requirements of the assignments and write excellent papers. So, why did she sometimes turn them in completed and on time, and other times either turn them in late or not at all?

I hated to give her the late grade when she turned them in late, but I knew I must stick to my rules for them to mean anything. When she did turn in assignments late, she never gave excuses. She simply handed the paper to me and apologized for her lateness. I attempted speaking with her to find a reason for her lateness and, perhaps, find a way to help her. Although friendly enough, and genuinely thankful for my interest, she never revealed her secret.

Before things went too far I e-mailed her mother asking for a meeting to discuss my concerns. I didn't tell her mother much in the e-mail, because I suspected apathy, or at least some lack of support. I received a return e-mail promptly, and she agreed to the meeting. Needless to say, this buoyed my spirits. I decided my suspicions were wrong and looked forward to the meeting to clear the air and help this girl.

It was a meeting I'll not soon forget. Her mother came to my room and sat in the chair next to my desk. I asked for her daughter to come with her, but neither she nor her father came. The mother sat quietly, not speaking. I worried she was angry with me for some reason and was carefully weighing the words she would use before speaking. I expressed my concerns, and when finished I inquired as to why neither her daughter nor her husband had come with her. She shifted uncomfortably in her seat before finally speaking quietly. Her daughter had been suffering from physical and mental abuse from her father. The mother was separated from him and had a court restraining order prohibiting him from coming within 100 yards of their daughter. He had violated that order and beaten the girl. This time she couldn't hide the bruises. She asked that her daughter be excused from classes for the next few days until her bruises could heal or be effectively covered with make-up. I felt my heart jump into my throat as I sat there in silence, fighting back the tears. Once I gathered myself together I told her how sorry I was for both her and her daughter, and that I could easily accommodate her needs.

The girl still missed an assignment from time to time and I still applied my rules, but she did begin to smile more while in my class. I hope she manages to make a good life for herself. Her mother never sent me anymore e-mails or called me, even though I e-mailed her from time to time to let her know of a late assignment.

Should I have done more? I did discuss the situation with our guidance counselor, who checked the story and found it to be correct. We agreed that the talent of this young student and her perseverance through such adversity would take her wherever she wanted to go. She has scars that may never go away, but they are her scars and, as her teacher, I can only provide the stable role model she needs, and go on teaching.

By the way, when this girl became a senior, she volunteered to tutor younger students. One of my responsibilities is to act as adviser to our chapter of the National Honor Society. The NHS student members tutor other students as a service to the school, and I coordinate that activity. This girl didn't make it into the

NHS chapter, but the fact that she wanted to help other students told me she was doing great.

What Is Parental Apathy?

You must continue learning about this, as no specific definition always applies. You must learn that "family" doesn't just mean the wholesome Nelsons from the idealistic 1950s show *The Adventures of Ozzie and Harriet*; sometimes, "family" simply consists of people who live together for some form of mutual benefit. You can't find out the family situation of all your students, so you must develop a sixth sense in this area. As you do this, remember the following:

- You aren't infallible.
- Your responsibility is to teach your students so learning takes place in your classroom.
- The kids aren't the only ones who aren't perfect; their parents aren't either.
- Whether or not you have kids of your own, you must understand that unless your students' parents also teach, they have knowledge and skills quite different from yours. Respect them for that.
- When meeting with parents, do not talk down to them, even if you know they have less education than you.
- Since you will probably never meet the truly apathetic parent, allow for the very real possibility that the homes of your students may in no way resemble what you consider normal.

Keeping all these points in mind will help you when you do run into a student from an apathetic household. As always, remember that your goal is to educate the student.

Apparent Apathy

You can easily confuse apparent apathy for the real thing. Apparent apathy simply defined means that, although the parent or parents love and want the best for their children, they have become so distracted they can't show it. This means you can't seem to get their attention on their child's needs no matter how hard you try.

Until otherwise proven wrong, you must treat apparent apathy as the real thing. In other words, while continuing with regular communications to the parents, make sure your students know you care about them as persons and want the best for them. Do this by making sure all your students know the rules of your classroom. Treat all of them with respect. Let them know your door is always open and that you are very approachable. They may need a soft place to land, but that doesn't mean you bend your educational rules just for them. And don't forget they are kids.

THE FEAR I have called; written notes for a student to take home; sent e-mails; and talked to the school counselor trying to get a meeting with the parents of one of my students, all to no avail. The young man has all the symptoms of either living in a family in trouble, or living on the streets. He comes to school dirty, sleepy, and hungry, and sleeps in my class, and he is failing. What else can I do? Or what else should I do?

THE SOLUTION It sounds like you are a very good teacher who loves her students. The first and most important thing you can do is not blame yourself for his circumstances. If you also have made tutoring services you know of available to him to help with his studies, you have pretty much run the gamut. You can't fix a home problem, but you should remain vigilant regarding his health, and watch for any signs of abuse. If you see unusual cuts or bruises or any shifts in his demeanor, you should let the school nurse and/or the counselor know. If your school has forms to complete when you have these kinds of concerns about a student, make sure you use them so your information will be properly channeled. And remember, your heart should be your guide. Don't listen to the skeptical teachers who have become cynical and have hardened their hearts.

LET'S SUMMARIZE . . .

❶ Apathy could be symptomatic of deeper problems in the home of the student. You must try to determine what you are actually dealing with before deciding how to handle it.

❷ You must provide the role model of a confident, caring, stable adult.

❸ Do not cease in your attempts to gain the attention of the parents of a student in trouble.

❹ Continue learning your subject, teaching methods, and about the psychology of the family.

CHAPTER 20

Will There Be Repercussions to My Disciplining?

While Chapter 7 addressed the overall legal liability of teachers, this chapter will extend that topic to the level of the fears specifically related to differences between helicopter parents and apathetic parents. It will address those fears from societal, legal, and practical viewpoints.

Societal Issues

There exists a whole raft of societal elements affecting your ability to teach. The first one that comes to mind relates to societal developments of both teaching and parenting. For example, back in the early days of public education, the one-room schoolhouse reigned supreme in most small towns and rural areas. The urban public schools were growing in size but were primarily neighborhood oriented due to methods of transportation. Teachers had no consistent educational background, and many had little formal education beyond the completion of high school. This essentially meant they had not been taught how to teach. They had to rely on their own studies to expand their teaching skills, and so there developed vast differences in knowledge levels within the overall society.

Discipline was both verbal and corporal. Society felt using physical forms of punishment changed student attitudes about misbehavior, thereby enhancing learning. If you caused trouble and disturbed the class you received a whack from the teacher and her discipline paddle. A quiet classroom meant a learning environment. Educators also felt the only way to remember important information was by memorization. Evaluative thought didn't enter into the picture. If a student could memorize facts and regurgitate them when asked, he had learned something.

"Times are a' changin'" as they say, and we have changed our view of disciplinary techniques and what they are supposed to accomplish. Our society went through a tumultuous period in the decade called "The Turbulent '60s," when society began to think using corporal punishment for disciplinary purposes was creating a society that believed the way to solve arguments or disagreements was to hit. The fear that society was becoming too violent grew, and so the rules of the game changed. Educators began to think that reasoning and explaining would do the job. If we only explained the rule and the consequences to the child, the correct behavior would result. The question of how to reason with a six-year-old, or even a thirteen-year-old child, didn't gain consideration.

The thinking that corporal punishment was detrimental evolved into thinking we had "spared the rod" and lost control. Since then modern science has discovered that the part of the brain that understands consequences of actions doesn't fully develop until about age twenty-one.

Now you must also deal with other societal issues such as blended families, families living below the poverty line, single-parent households, both parents working two jobs, very rich families in which money supplants parental love, and more. It's your job to navigate these ever-changing times with an attitude that keeps the child first, no matter the type of home they come from.

Legal Issues

Various states' legislatures have considered eliminating joint and several liability with regard to school systems. Doing this would mean that when the court finds two defendants guilty of the negligence causing injury, but one defendant is insolvent, the injured party would not be fully compensated by the other defendant. Current bills only intend to apply this to non-monetary damages, yet, generally, a large portion of a child plaintiff's damages are non-monetary.

Twenty-three states allow corporal punishment, and some even maintain immunity for the teacher. The states where corporal punishment is currently legal are:

Alabama

Arizona

Arkansas

Colorado

Florida

Georgia

Idaho

Indiana

Kansas

Kentucky

Louisiana

Mississippi

Missouri

New Mexico

North Carolina

Ohio

Oklahoma

Pennsylvania

Rhode Island (legal, but banned by every school board
in the state)

South Carolina

Tennessee

Texas

Wyoming

Here are some examples of the corporal punishment taking
place in our schools:

In 2000, a Georgia coach witnessed a fourteen-year-old hitting a teammate with a device he had weighted with a metal
padlock, so the coach dug it out of the boy's gym bag and
struck him with it, blinding the boy's left eye.

In 1997, a teacher from Ohio tied a second-grader to his desk
so he would stop moving around.

A seventeen-year-old female suffered from internal vaginal bleeding due to a paddling she received as punishment for fighting in Ohio in 1997.

In 1990, a coach in Texas held a starter pistol to a fourteen-year-old boy's body while threatening to hang him as a method to get the boy to focus.

In 1993, a Texas teacher struck an elementary boy with a stick, causing him to defecate in his pants.

The United States Supreme Court ruled that under the U.S. Constitution corporal punishment is permissible, and yet twenty-seven states have prohibited it. The legal environment seems murky at best. Everything I can find leads me to conclude that corporal punishment has no place in schools. Your best option from a legal standpoint, and I'm no attorney, is to apply a punishment that equates to the offense. Make sure the students know the rules. And, in compliance with the Center of Justice, apply your punishment equally without discrimination based on sex, race, or any other factors.

Practical Issues

Punishment for committing offenses that deter from the learning environment in your classroom must be applied. You have a responsibility to teach all the students in your classroom as well as provide proper adult supervision of their activities. Safety must always be an important consideration in evaluating the degree of the offense. If you are teaching a class that includes lab work, and that lab work requires the use of chemicals, sharp tools, heavy tools, or other instruments with which they can injure either themselves or others, you have an obligation to require they use these in a safe manner.

Apathetic Versus Helicopter Parents' Reactions

Will you have a higher degree of legal liability when dealing with apathetic parents than with helicopter parents? It's not a matter of degree. Your liability for negligent actions carries the same weight. The difference surfaces when a legal action is brought against you.

The best way to avoid having these kinds of problems is to always treat your students fairly, make every use of your teaching skills to create a learning environment, and stay in regular contact with the parents. If they feel like partners in the education of their child, they will support your efforts when the child is out of school. But, how do you know when you've done this well? Feedback. Unfortunately, with the apathetic parents you may never receive any communication, and you will receive so much from the hovering parents that pleasing them seems an impossible task.

You and the parents both have a supervisory responsibility; however, you've been trained and they haven't. There should not be any overlap of this authority, and, with apathetic parents, there won't be. Unfortunately, they more than likely aren't doing their job outside of school either. The helicopter parents, on the other hand, may be managing the life of their child so tightly that it not only encroaches on the school day, but usurps your ability to provide proper supervision.

The apathetic parents will cause surprise, and sometimes problems, when they finally do decide to get in contact, usually when something bad happens, like their child receiving a failing grade. You need to continue taking every step to communicate with them even though your efforts seem to fall on deaf ears. You also need to document your efforts.

The hovering parents who become so involved in their child's life that they interfere with your teaching create quite a different problem. By the time they decide to file any kind of legal action against you or your school you will have seen it coming, just by paying attention to their actions. With the apathetic parents you long for communication, whereas with the hoverers you just wish they would go away and let you teach.

Your principal can really help you deal with helicopter parents. The more she communicates with these parents, the more comfortable the parent becomes with the safety of his child, if in elementary school, or the excellent learning environment, if in high school.

The level and type of communication within the school community is a function of the parent base. The parental group may have differences in social class or homogeneity of social class. The makeup of the group affects attendance and function of the parent organization and, therefore, how much support the parents provide to the school. Parents volunteering as teacher assistants, coaches, or fundraisers will mean less interference with your actual ability to teach. Be sure to try to involve parents of all social classes in your classroom and school activities. If circumstances cannot allow them to make scheduled events, see if you can work the next event around their schedules.

Finally, you can improve your communication with parents through certain Internet sites established for parent/teacher collaboration. As I've already mentioned, you can make use of e-mail, an Internet blog, or your own website in order to keep in constant communication with your students' parents. Take advantage of the help that technology provides.

THE FEAR I have some kids in my classroom who only respond to corporal punishment. If I don't give them a paddling when they misbehave, they become so disruptive I lose control of my class. I teach eighth grade and have thirty-five students in my classroom all day. I can't afford to take the time to reason with them.

THE SOLUTION You have two problems. The most obvious to you is the size of the class. If you had no more than twenty-four, most of these problems would disappear. However, the bigger problem you may have is lack of good classroom management. You need to establish every day what they will achieve, how they will achieve it, and then you need to give them periodic breaks. If you do this, they will be too busy to cause trouble. The breaks will give their brains an opportunity to absorb the material covered as well as to rest.

LET'S SUMMARIZE . . .

❶ Apathy and aggression are often derived from societal, legal, or practical issues.

❷ Legal issues will arise no matter the social class, but their manifestation will depend on the focus of the parents.

❸ Practical methods of dealing with the students in your school provide the answer to minimal legal involvement.

❹ You have a duty to supervise as well as teach.

PART IV

External Fears

You have no control over what happens

outside your classroom

CHAPTER 21

Are My Students Going to Be Able to Compete?

Your fear of the United States falling behind the rest of the world has been realized. (If you did not have a fear of American public schools falling behind those of the rest of the world, you should have.) The point of this book is to rid you of your fears by recognizing them, help you to understand that most teachers have the same fears, and then provide information that will help eliminate or greatly reduce your fears. However, it doesn't seem that this fear will be easily laid to rest. American independence is inextricably linked to a healthy American economy and a level of education superior to all others. I am about to take you on a roller coaster ride that is only going downhill. Fasten your seat belts.

A Measure of the Economy

The United States has started to take a nosedive. Need proof? Check out the following.

1. The concept of the government providing for all our needs is a myth. You now work three times longer per year to pay all your taxes. This means paying more to the government than

you pay for food, housing, and clothing combined. Social spending by the government has grown fourteen times faster than the economy from 1947 to 2006. This reduces your freedom of choice. Do you want the government to control 44 percent of our economy?

2. There has been a 71 percent decline in education productivity since 1960, meaning huge increases in spending on education, but with a declining quality output. This can be illustrated by changing the measurement criteria for the SAT instead of correcting poor quality. The result is that more and more colleges are forced to teach remedial courses that should have been taught in high school. According to the *Grandfather Economic Report* series:

    The U.S. Department of Education NAEP testing of 300,000 students in all 50 states in 2005 showed 82% of 12th graders not proficient in science, worse than 10 years earlier.

3. America's total debt (that's all of us, not just the federal government) has reached $48 trillion, up from $5 trillion in 1957, and this is adjusted for inflation. The debt is increasing more than two times faster than income.

4. According to the International Trade Report, America has gone from a creditor nation to a debtor nation, increasing debt by some $2.2 billion per day. Ours is an economy mostly based on services and spending in excess of production and savings. This means we have become more and more dependent on other countries, which will ultimately negatively affect our living standards.

5. We consume three times more oil than we produce. In addition, our natural gas reserves are falling, while imports

are rising. Both of these threaten prosperity and national security.

Education Quality

Since 1947, education quality has declined 71 percent (without consideration of the costs of remedial education in colleges to make up for primary and secondary deficiencies). There seems to be an inverse relationship between spending on education and quality of result. That could simply mean there is something seriously wrong with the system. Here are some interesting items as food for thought:

1. More than 44 percent of college freshmen reported they had an A average in high school, yet many require remedial help in English and math.

2. The U.S. Department of Education reported in 2001 that two-thirds of our fourth-graders read below grade level, but that private-school students performed better than those in public schools.

3. A professor representing the American Association of Physics Teachers reported in 2001 that 85 percent of middle school science textbooks were so full of errors and inaccuracies that they were unacceptable. The professor also reported that honors high school textbooks were no more difficult than an eighth-grade reader of fifty years ago.

4. The Organisation of Economic Cooperation and Development (OECD) in April 2001 reported that 60 percent of Americans aged sixteen to twenty-five are "functionally illiterate," meaning they couldn't properly fill out a form, and that on the simple numerical test they scored at the bottom of all industrialized nations.

5. There have been a number of reports between 1997 and 2001 indicating the homeschooled kids scored 70 percent higher than public school kids on standardized national achievement tests, regardless of race, economic status, or regulation levels.

6. A recent Florida study revealed that 70 percent of high school graduates need remedial courses when entering community college.

7. A 2002 report indicated that poor inner-city Cleveland students with vouchers who selected Catholic schools had a graduation rate of 99.6 percent, compared to only a 30 percent graduation rate in local public schools.

8. In 2005 China produced four times more BS engineering degrees than did the United States. A Nobel Prize–winning scientist from Rice University predicts that, by 2010, 90 percent of all PhD physical scientists and engineers in the world will be Asians living in Asia.

9. In 2006, according to the *Grandfather Economic Report* series, 65 percent of American twelfth-graders were not proficient in reading, which was worse than in 1992 when the National Assessment of Educational Progress first started its assessments.

Following are some questions from an eighth-grade final exam written in 1895:

- Name the parts of speech and define those that have no modifications.
- What is punctuation?
- Give rules for principal marks of punctuation.
- Name and define the fundamental rules of arithmetic.
- A wagon box is 2 feet deep, 10 feet long, and 3 feet wide. How many bushels of wheat will it hold?

- Find the bank discount on $300 for 90 days (no grace) at 10 percent.
- Give the epochs into which U.S. History is divided. Relate the causes and results of the Revolutionary War.
- Name events connected with the following dates: 1607, 1620, 1800, 1849, and 1865.
- Use the following correctly in sentences: cite, site, sight, fane, fain, feign, vane, vein, raze, raise, rays.
- What is climate?
- Upon what does climate depend?
- Of what use are rivers? Of what use is the ocean?
- Name and describe the following: Monrovia, Odessa, Denver, Manitoba, Hecla, Yukon, St. Helena, Juan Fernandez, Aspinwall, and Orinoco.
- Describe the movements of the earth.
- Give the inclination of the earth.

These are just some of the total of 48 questions. See how many of these you can answer. I did an informal survey of seniors at our school and they missed two-thirds of these. I wonder how well eighth graders across the country would do. My guess is, not very well.

If you really have an interest, go to the following website and enjoy: *http://skyways.lib.ks.us/kansas/genweb/* (the KSGenWeb Project).

Education Worldwide

I have a friend from India who is a computer systems engineer. He has told me that the education system in India is so competitive that he, even though a straight-A student through elementary, secondary, and undergraduate college, was not accepted to a master's program in computer engineering in India. So, he applied to MIT and was accepted immediately. Although I sometimes have difficulty understanding his English, he never misunderstands mine. I was a top executive for an insurance company, and we hired him as a systems engineer. I spent about four hours lecturing him about insurance. He took no notes as I spoke, but periodically asked the kind of questions that told me he was grasping everything.

I worked with him for the following three years and never once suspected he had no prior training in the business. I studied the business for many years to get where I was, and he amazed me with his comprehension. I later learned that the basic studies he had taken in high school and college allowed him to understand my lecture. I'm afraid that solid basis is what our education system is failing to provide. This is one of the reasons American business is compelled to go overseas to hire the work force it needs. Sure, the cost of that work force is less than it is here, but other countries also provide the necessary educational background for the skills the businesses need.

THE FEAR I teach high school Spanish and in spite of it being a required subject, the students I get seem to make very little effort toward understanding why they need to learn this. I have made trips to many Latin American countries where Spanish is spoken and brought back wonderful pictures and artifacts of those cultures to share with my students. What can I do that I haven't already tried?

THE SOLUTION Let me share a personal experience that will help. Several years ago while still in the corporate world I accepted an assignment to a foreign country where I didn't speak the language. My wife and I took an intensive conversational course in the language. From the first day no one at the school spoke English with us. We were not given a text book nor any written instructions in English. Needless to say we struggled. Then when we arrived in the foreign country I (my wife had a family to care for) began taking another intensive class and read newspapers and watched local television programs. It was an exhausting experience, but in six months I was fluent conversationally. What a wonderful feeling it is to hold a conversation in a foreign language.

Obviously, you can't go to the same extreme as the language school we attended, but the point of the story is the reward we received in learning a new language. If you make the value of what you are teaching clear to your students, they will want to learn.

LET'S SUMMARIZE . . .

❶ You must have a healthy fear of the American education system falling behind the rest of the world.

❷ The economic situation and our independence as a democratic society depend on our education system.

❸ The American economy seems to be in a free fall.

❹ The American public education system has already taken a nosedive and needs drastic change to pull it out before it crashes.

❺ I repeat, you must have a healthy fear of the American education system falling behind the rest of the world.

CHAPTER 22

How Does the Neighborhood Affect My School?

They just don't seem to care. You'd think that by the time they were seventeen or eighteen years old they would begin to see a bigger picture. You'd think they would actually begin to see the value in what you try to teach them every day. But they don't, and you become even more frustrated at the seeming powerlessness of the teaching profession. This not only worries you but frightens you as you recognize the needs of an ever-shrinking world. You know the isolationist past will remain in the past, and we Americans must think globally. But all they care about is what's going on in their neighborhood. They become so wrapped up in trivial issues that they do not seem to care about the greater ones. It's your job to make them care. Show them that no matter where they're from, they should care.

J. Paul Getty, founder of Getty Oil Company, once said, "No one can possibly achieve any real and lasting success or 'get rich' in business by being a conformist."

Think about Betty Naomi Friedan, cofounder of the National Organization of Women, who wrote the first book addressing how women could lead fulfilled lives outside of the home and child-rearing. Or think about Andrew Carnegie, who had come here as a dirt-poor Scottish lad and became an industrialist and multimillionaire. He became yet more famous as a philanthropist because of his feeling that businesses and successful businesspeople had an obligation to give back to their communities. Recently Will Smith starred in *The Pursuit of Happyness*, which is the story of Chris Gardner, who went from living with his young son in subway trains and sleeping in public bathrooms to being a multimillionaire stockbroker. He became homeless after losing his job, but was determined to become successful and to make a good life. Red Octane struggled until he finally became recognized and wealthy only after publishing and selling the first music-based computer game. Jay Thiessens grew up illiterate in Nevada and now is a multimillionaire businessman. Sam Walton turned his love for flying a small plane and the marketing involved in retail sales into the largest retail store operation in the United States (Wal-Mart). And I want to mention one more person before ending this list. That person is Oprah Winfrey, the highly successful television talk show host who came from very meager beginnings.

The point is, don't give up, and do make every effort to understand the neighborhood where your students live. They may have two very different worlds to deal with.

A Personal Story

I grew up in a loving, but relatively poor family. I don't mean to imply that we lived like Chris Gardner, or that I faced any sort of racial issues like Oprah Winfrey, but my father only went as far as the eighth grade because he was needed to help out in his father's landscape and nursery business. Although Dad never cared much for formal schooling, he would learn whatever he needed to accomplish his goals. For example, he taught himself how to make blueprints, and how to calculate the amount and cost of building materials necessary to build the home where I spent most of my youth. He used those figures to obtain the financing he needed for the project. He learned what he needed to know about plumbing, electrical work, and carpentry to build the house. Then, when he wasn't working at the local steel mill, he built the house himself. I get tired thinking about the strenuous steel-mill work he did, after which he added another four to six hours laying cement block or cutting studs to the right length for walls, or painting, or any of the numerous jobs needed to build our home. He seemed to work around the clock on some days. When he was working the night shift at the mill he would come home in the morning and go right to work on the house.

My mother always worked at some part-time job to help out with the household expenses, but she always had time to take us to school and to other activities. She, like my father, didn't graduate from high school. When she was in her junior year she was asked and expected to go to the aid of an aunt suffering from tuberculosis. Mom lived a very meager existence as part of a large family in Kentucky. She hated leaving school and always encouraged my sister, brother, and me in our educational pursuits. It is with this background that I decided to include this chapter in this book. My older sister was the first in either my mother's or my father's family to graduate from college. Seeing how proud they all were of her, I too, went on to college, as did my younger brother. The fact that we grew up in a lower-middle-class society and lived in a neighborhood some would have referred to as hillbilly heaven, because most of our neighbors came from the poor hills of Kentucky where there was no work for them, didn't stop us from moving on. Most of the men worked at the same mill as my dad. Although we had farmers as neighbors behind our home, if we looked out our front window we could see the black smoke rising from the steel-making furnaces, or feel the earth shaking as a thimble slowly turned on its huge spindles, dumping slag into the hard Ohio clay.

I know our country was founded on the concept of having a classless society. Our Founding Fathers wanted nothing to do with kingdoms and royalty. However, the free society they created, which fosters individual initiative, has become a financial-class society. These classes will naturally migrate toward one another, and some will even find themselves trapped.

My background of living in a working-class household in which my father did shift work that carried with it a fairly high exposure to danger and personal injury caused me to want to bring out another class of society, one that influences the basic thinking of its offspring and your students.

Recently the news media made us aware of a coal mine disaster in West Virginia, and another in Minnesota. Many of my colleagues and friends wondered why anyone would do such dangerous work. The answer is that they are trapped in a social cycle of generations of families tied to that way of life.

During my business career I started an operation in West Virginia. The man I hired to manage it came from a coal-mining family. His father died from black lung disease, a form of cancer caused from breathing in coal dust over long periods of time. He really knew the mining business and had great business contacts throughout the state, and those were two great attributes. The best qualities this man had to offer took some time to discover. They were his honesty, integrity, and business acumen, qualities rarely found in one person today. He managed to break out of the mining cycle, but he couldn't leave his family, all of whom lived in the little town where I wanted to set up business.

It was because of this man and the lessons he imparted to me about the coal-mining business that I bought and read a book titled *Coal Miners' Wives*. In this book, Carol A. B. Giesen very vividly illustrates life in the old coal-mining camp towns, which was very similar to life in today's mining towns. The man in the family works shift work, like my dad did, and so has great difficulty sleeping, making the work even more dangerous. We all need regular sleep-and-wake patterns to properly rest our minds. Without this, the mind can play tricks as it tries to get the needed rest. As a result of their tiredness, the miners sometimes have accidents that cause the loss of limbs, or even their lives. Of course, the work itself carries with it the ever-present potential of an explosion or mine collapse. The women have to stay at home to be there to comfort their husbands, and to take care of the children. They have difficulty taking jobs themselves, even part-time jobs. The shift work and long hours worked by the men leave them unable to provide any sort of household help to their wives.

You would think that the children would want to escape that lifestyle. You would think the mothers and fathers would encourage their escape. But, once the boys reach the age when they could begin working in the mine, usually sixteen or seventeen, they often drop out of school and take pride in doing what their daddy did. Rarely do they leave the town. Usually they will continue living at home, even if they marry, until they can find an available house in the town to rent. Thus the cycle continues.

Coal-mining work brings a constant fear into the home. The wife never knows when she will receive a phone call informing her that there has been a mine collapse, or that her husband has had an accident. That fear creates tremendous anxiety to the point of actually preventing her from leaving the house.

Households Striking Fear

There are other professions that bring similar fears into the household. Among such workers are police officers, firemen, oil rig workers, and commercial fishermen. Military families suffer not only the anxiety of a loved one possibly being lost in war, but long absences due to overseas assignments. Like the coal-mining families, the people who work in these fields tend to live together in the same neighborhoods. Their reasons may simply be economic, but they also result from human nature, from wanting to live with people with whom they feel comfortable, people who know and understand them.

If your students don't seem to care, it may be because they lack the maturity to care, or it may be they really don't see school as relevant for them.

School Is So Different

Schools should have at their core developing an educated citizenry. By that very focus they will be unlike the neighborhoods and people I have been describing. The kids literally leave their world, the place where they feel the most comfortable, and enter yours. You must find ways to relate the two.

Let's look at the other financial classes for a few minutes. Many of the kids who come from the so-called privileged households have been pampered with material things they don't even need, told by well-meaning parents they can do anything or be anything they want. Then, when they enter your room, where everyone is equal and has to work to succeed, they sometimes freak out. Alternatively, they may make themselves even more untouchable, creating real tension with the rest of the student population.

Then there is the great middle class. Although the kids in this class will generally make up the largest percentage of the student population in most classrooms (except in distressed urban areas or some private schools), they also fit the mold of the students causing the least amount of controversy. Therefore, I will move on to the students of poverty and broken homes.

You can't expect this latter group of kids to have computers in their homes, or even have homes in some cases. Because so many of these students live with families that do not value education, they will find little support at home for most of your educational projects. They don't have parents who go off to work or are at home on a regular basis. Some have illegal drugs in their homes, or see it sold on the streets of their neighborhoods, or sell or use drugs themselves. They see horrible crimes committed on their doorsteps almost daily. These students will vary in classroom participation from none, because they are sleeping, to nearly manic in their demands on your attention. These will be special cases, and you will need to spend time with your school counselor making sure your efforts comply with the Individualized Education Programs (IEPs) set for them. School may actually be providing the safe place to land that home should provide. This doesn't mean, however, that they will be model students. Remember, it's hard to concentrate when you're hungry.

Because you know you have kids that fit somewhere in the spectrum from rich to poor and from structured historical entrapment to the average kid, you must find a way to accommodate all of them in your classroom. Establish a common respect among them to develop a good learning environment.

THE FEAR I can deal with the snobby kid who makes fun of the poor kid, or the kid from the rough neighborhood who frightens others, but how do I manage to teach the same lesson to all of them?

THE SOLUTION You don't. That is, you don't need to teach all of them at the same level. As a matter of fact, if you have a kid on an IEP who needs tests read to him, or who always needs extra time to do assignments, you must schedule his work load so he can handle it. If you don't do this you will lose students. It demands a superhuman effort on your part, but isn't that why you became a teacher?

LET'S SUMMARIZE . . .

❶ People may not need a lot of formal education to be successful, because many do not, but it certainly increases the possibility.

❷ Be aware that many homes have stressful environments due to dangerous occupations that make learning in school difficult. Also, recognize that your best efforts may fail because of traditional family class values.

❸ School by its very nature provides an environment different from the students' homes.

❹ The kid from the home exposed to a high crime element needs special treatment.

CHAPTER 23

What Do I Do about Drugs in My School?

I'll bet you worry about the effect of drugs on your students. You have some who seem to have different personalities from day to day. However, what about the greater fear of teachers taking drugs? Teachers are supposed to be good role models for students. How should you and your fellow teachers tackle drug issues before tackling those of your students? Let's see.

Teachers and Drugs

There isn't any teacher reading this book who doesn't realize that illegal drugs or inappropriate use of legal drugs can destroy his or her life. There are also teachers reading this who have become addicted to either legal or illegal drugs. Let's take a look at legal drugs first because of the insidious potential they have to take over your life.

Legal Drugs

I understand that human beings can only stand a certain level of pain and, if it goes beyond that point, the brain shuts it off. Unfortunately, that reaction can have devastating effects. That's why surgeons give us painkillers as well as anesthesia during a surgical procedure. Just being asleep doesn't rid us of the pain of surgery. Without the proper drugs the body would react by attacking the source of the pain, thus inhibiting the healing process. Painkillers, on the other hand, get rid of that reaction, calming the mind and allowing the healing process to take over.

There have been hundreds and probably thousands of documented circumstances in which people who started taking a prescription painkiller after surgery became "hooked." The relief they needed for the pain was replaced by the high they got once the pain subsided. The change from healing to high was so subtle they hardly noticed, but "hooked" they were. Some even became so hooked they increased their dosage by finding several doctors to prescribe the drug, allowing them to go higher and higher into their cloud of oblivion.

If you have a healthy fear of this happening to you, be grateful, because that fear is a protection for you. It is one fear you don't want to lose. Just don't get carried away to the point where you refuse taking a painkiller when you really need it.

With the inefficient operation of health care in this country, it's no wonder people get hooked on legal drugs. By "inefficient" I mean the steps that sometimes are required to find the treatment you need. It starts by having enough knowledge of medicine and your body to come up with an idea of what to do. Assuming that over-the-counter remedies won't do the job, you contact your family physician for an appointment. The next step could be to make an appointment with a specialist. Assuming you get to see this person before something worse happens, you may receive a prescription for some sort of medication that may relieve the pain or may actually fix the problem. If the problem is not corrected, the specialist may send you to a surgeon, who will determine whether a surgical procedure is required. Subsequently, and before the actual surgery, you may need physical therapy, and then the surgery, followed by more therapy. These treatments involve different medical professionals, each of whom may prescribe different drugs to help you. All of this could result in your feeling the need for more and more medication, which often includes Valium, Vicodin, oxycodone, amphetamines, tizanidine, and on and on.

Please don't get the idea that I'm down on our health care system, because I'm not. This example just illustrates how easily you can become dependent on drugs that alter your perception of reality. They may give you energy beyond your physical ability, or make you sleepy or at least drowsy enough that you shouldn't drive or try to concentrate on a lesson plan. Or they can make you irritable, causing you to alter your normal disciplinary methods and confuse your students.

But, what if you really need these drugs? No question; you use them. You must do what your physician tells you or you won't get the results she expects, and may even worsen your condition.

How about Weight Control?

Weight control and losing unwanted pounds seems to have become an obsession in this country. This seems especially so if you pay attention to TV or newspaper or magazine ads. How many of you have picked up a magazine directed to a female audience that isn't filled with ads for weight-loss plans, exercise plans, or surgical procedures to tuck skin, suck out fat, and pinch off or clamp shut a part of the digestive system? Do you believe those before-and-after pictures featuring rail-thin women in bikinis whose breasts still fill D-cup bras? Have you ever heard of airbrushing?

And, if you like to read sports magazines that are directed at the males, what about those ads for building bulk or muscle mass? Look at those "after" pictures with those six-pack abs on a man who looks like he's nearing fifty. Do those men really manage to burn off all the middle-aged, gravity-managed stomach fat to attain rock-hard abdominal muscles without help from a photographic artist? Yet, the advertisers know that if we see these advertisements often enough, even the most cerebral of human beings will succumb and give their product a try.

So, down this path you go. You no longer need self-control or discipline to look like an Adonis or Halle Berry or Heidi Klum. Not so long ago, a highly touted weight-loss drug called phen-fen was taken off the market because of its link to high blood pressure. Then there are Topamax and Zonegran, which do cause weight loss; however, they calm the nerves and cause drowsiness, even a feeling of disorientation or zombie-like stupor, because they actually are intended for use as antiseizure medications. Since you feel so sluggish from these drugs you need to get a doctor to prescribe an amphetamine to get you back up. Amphetamines not only increase your potential for high blood pressure but are known to cross-addict to cocaine. You don't want to go there.

THE FEAR I've heard a couple of students make remarks about another teacher being on drugs. At first, I didn't even bother to acknowledge them, thinking it was just the kids exaggerating and making fun of her. However, I started to notice a change in her behavior and think their accusations may be true. But I don't want to jump to conclusions and make allegations against a fellow teacher.

THE SOLUTION It's important not to jump to conclusions. You should not just go off the words of your students, but you should follow up first with the teacher. Ask her how's she's feeling and if anything's wrong. She could be acting distant and out of the ordinary for a number of reasons. However, if after your conversation you still feel there is something wrong with the way she is acting, you should report it to an administrator.

LET'S SUMMARIZE . . .

❶ You must manage the legal drugs prescribed by your doctors.

❷ You can get hooked on painkillers, uppers, downers, sleep aids, and on and on.

❸ The bigger problem could actually result from trying to look like a supermodel or weightlifter.

❹ Study any medicine before taking it. Know all the uses and side effects and especially its addiction potential.

❺ You can't hide your moods from your students, but you can ruin your ability to teach because of them.

CHAPTER 24

Are My Students Safe on Their Way Home?

If you have been in this teaching business for many years, do you wonder where all the pedophiles came from? If new to this business, do you wonder what you've gotten yourself into? Will you become the next target of an accusation? Has our society always had this form of sexual perversion? Do you wonder if there really are more occurrences involving this horrible abuse of children, or has the fear of it become so pervasive that the adults misinterpret a child's imagination of such an event? Whether real or imagined, this may well be one of the greatest fears entering your classroom and lurking behind those innocent eyes looking back at you.

One of the first frightening experiences I had after entering teaching involved one of my freshman female students. I had been teaching at the high school level for only about two months when this effusive young girl came up to me as I stood in the hall between classes, watching the kids move from classrooms to their lockers, exchange books and papers, and go on to their next class. I remember thinking how much energy seemed to surge through that hallway, and mildly wishing some of it could somehow transfer to adults. Suddenly this young girl rushed to me and, while giving me a hug, thanked me for something I had taught in class earlier that day. I froze like a deer in headlights, arms plastered to my sides. I managed to respond that I was glad she got something out of it, but my mind raced forward several years into a courtroom seeing another student on the witness stand testifying that I had, indeed, improperly touched that girl. My mind's eye saw my teaching career crumbling, destroyed by an impulsive, well-meaning child. Then, just as quickly as she had grabbed me, she released me and ran on to another class.

. My immediate reaction made me feel miserable. I love children and have a grandchild who is older than that girl, so I really wanted to return the hug showing my love, but fear overruled my grandparental or parental instinct. What a pity.

I realize this incident resulted from an innocent, emotional teenage girl. You who teach elementary school children have situations like this daily. Children need to learn to express their emotions in proper ways, but we mustn't forget they are children. The part of their brain that recognizes that their actions have consequences is a long way from being developed. We also need to understand that touch is our first language. Many studies have shown that babies need frequent holding and stroking by the gentle hands of an adult caregiver.

Many European orphanages had no-touch policies to avoid the spread of infections as long ago as during World War I. Ninety percent of babies under the age of two in the institutions studied there died even though they had adequate food and shelter. A later study in Bellevue Hospital in New York City, where every baby was picked up and held several times a day, showed that fewer than 10 percent of the babies died. But now, because of the seeming surge in pedophilia, you must always think carefully before touching a student. You will encounter many occasions when your heart suffers from a losing struggle with your mind. You well know those strong emotional tugs by your heart telling you that a child suffering from heartbreak needs a hug from a caring teacher.

Your mind drags out the memory of that last lecture during an in-service, when you heard all those awful things that could happen to you if you did hug that child, and so you restrain yourself. How on earth did these complicated interpersonal relationships happen? Is pedophilia the problem, or is it child abuse? The current theory doesn't support family or societal causes, but rather an incurable form of mental illness. So, rather than trying to find ways to cure it to help the children, you must look into the deeper implications of child abuse. I believe the answer to the question of where they all come from lies there.

You also need to understand that no one really knows whether this problem is a recent phenomenon or if it has gone on for generations but wasn't publicized. Due to the possibility that the allegations of childhood sexual abuse are difficult to prove, and the ease with which a professional adult can intentionally or unintentionally lead a child, any statistics covering enough years for credibility are suspect. Simply stated, this means that child abuse and pedophilia may not actually be increasing. The raw numbers should not necessarily lead you to ask why there seem to be so many pedophiles now, when they didn't seem to be around a generation or more ago.

The Many Forms of Child Abuse

The current theories about pedophilia tell us that the sufferer cannot help himself or herself. Some suggest that therapy will help them cope and control their urges, much as it does for an alcoholic, but will not stop the desire. The children in your classroom who have suffered sexual abuse more often than not were not the victims of a pedophile. You should also understand that sufferers of poverty or sexual abuse do not become the perpetrators of these heinous acts. I have found no standard profile for juvenile sex offenders but, according to the Child Welfare Information Gateway and its reports from various studies, many such offenders have "weak social skills, behavior problems, learning disabilities, and depression." The same source says that adult offenders "are heterogeneous and attempts to identify common characteristics have not been successful. However, psychopathic and substance abuse disorders in adult offenders may predict recidivism." Fortunately, some treatment programs, with their goals of increasing understanding of the victims and decreasing deviant sexual arousal, have reduced the rate of crimes.

According to figures released by the Child Welfare League, nearly 80 percent of child abusers were the parents, and of these nearly 90 percent were the biological parents. More than half were Caucasian, and nearly 58 percent were women. Although from 1990 to 2001 the numbers of child abuse victims increased from 798,318 to 903,089, the percentage of abused children in the child population remained the same (1.24 percent, or 12.4 per 1,000 children). On the other hand, if you look at the number of children where abuse was reported, you will find that the number increased from 669,000 in 1976 to 2,694,000 in 1991. I tend to place more importance on the percentage of child victims from 1990 to 2001 because the reporting laws and associated public awareness programs had changed dramatically before that period. In 1963 only about 150,000 children of abuse were reported; this increased to the 1976 number of 669,000. Keep in mind that these reports include not only sexual abuse, but also other forms of both physical and emotional abuse to children of all ages.

What about Child Care Professionals and Teachers?

If you or any other teacher or day care person suffers an accusation of child abuse, it will hit the news as if you were a serial killer. Don't forget that the public holds us to a higher standard. Also don't forget that it actually happens. Rational public thought can fail quickly, fading into mass hysteria just as it did during the witchcraft trials back in 1692 in Salem, Massachusetts. Emotional response often prevents rational thought.

It's important to remember that many accusations of child abuse are false. Many courts suspect that the parent who makes the accusation is lying because the media has created the image of the mother making false accusations of paternal child abuse to hurt the father. On the other hand, most courts take very seriously their responsibility to protect the children in these cases.

I specialized in unusual and highly risky insurance coverages for a number of years during my long insurance career. In the late 1980s I began to experience a rapid increase in the demand to provide day care centers with insurance to protect them financially in the event they were accused of abusing or harming the children in their care. I remember wondering, when this demand first began, why the centers couldn't get the insurance from the regular insurance market as they always had. I researched the news reports and came across the classic case that started it all, the now infamous McMartin case in Los Angeles Superior Court.

The prosecution alleged that Virginia McMartin, 78, and her daughter, granddaughter, grandson, and three instructors had sexually abused and exposed the children in their care to satanic ritual abuse in their preschool in Manhattan Beach, California. Later the court dropped the charges against five of the seven, and the last two were acquitted in 1990, but not before the ugliness of such a trial and out-of-court actions became a media sensation. The defense took the position that the children fantasized about the alleged events. The mother who first complained was subsequently found dead of an apparent suicide. Anatomically correct dolls were used by psychiatrists to gain details of events from the children. The children exposed hideous satanic rituals which involved making them drink animal blood and witness the killing of animals, and on and on. The insurance community began quickly shrinking away from providing any coverage for day care centers and the possibility of the enormous legal fees that could result. It seemed the only winners in these kinds of cases were the lawyers. Any allegation of this sort could potentially ruin the day care operators; expose the parents to enormous anxiety; cause the victims future years of mental anguish; and result in the creation of punitive laws affecting all educational operations.

Now that those years are behind us, we know what can happen and that as a result we educators have a laundry list of rules to adhere to in addition to applying common sense and restraint of our natural emotions when it comes to dealing with our charges. Remember that the focus of the fear of pedophilia in your classroom is on the child and not the perpetrator. The best you can do to help protect the children in your care is to teach them that child molesters are not necessarily the ugly men in strange cars on dark streets, but possibly people they know and trust. Only a very small percentage of child molesters use physical force, so the child should run, scream, or make a scene. And, finally, make sure your students know they can talk to you, because many times the molestation occurs in the home. The victim needs someone who listens, and then reports it so the right people will take the right action to help the child.

THE FEAR One of my students is a fifteen-year-old girl who has become withdrawn. She used to be one of the popular girls in our school. Now she just sits and looks at me with a glassy stare. She doesn't participate in any discussions either in small groups or in the class as a whole. I've always been told to look for sudden changes in a child's personality or sudden weight loss as indications of drug or child abuse. The problem with this girl is that whatever changed her didn't cause any sudden transformation, so I'm confused about what to do, if anything. The other teachers say they don't see it.

THE SOLUTION It sounds like the problem could be either drug or child abuse. You may be witnessing the lows of drug abuse, or depression brought on by an abusive parent or other adult. Remember the insidious nature of these issues makes them hard to detect with a high degree of certainty. So, you must communicate your concerns to her parents and to the school guidance counselor and principal, and you must do it quickly. Either of these situations could deteriorate rapidly. It's better to be wrong and risk upsetting her parents and your principal than having further harm come to her.

LET'S SUMMARIZE . . .

❶ Child abuse didn't just begin during your era. The legal environment has changed and society has become more aware because reporting of this hideous crime has improved.

❷ Rather than limiting your definition of "abuse" to sexual abuse, you must have an awareness of the overall issue of child abuse. Only then will you understand the fears children bring to your classroom.

❸ The children in your care do not transfer their abuse to you, but they also are not able to leave it outside your classroom or at home.

❹ Be aware that the media sensationalizes any allegations of child abuse involving a teacher or child care professional.

❺ By teaching children how to recognize, resist, and report child abuse or abusers, you teach the children how to protect themselves.

CHAPTER 25

Terrorism and My Classroom

Ever have days when you just wish people could get along? Is it in our human nature to want what someone else has, or to fear other people's lifestyles so much we must either take that coveted possession or kill them?

Some would call me a Pollyanna for thinking the world is filled with good people who seek happiness. I do, indeed, feel that way, but by reading and watching the news I temper a potential for allowing that thinking to carry me to a state of unrealistic euphoria. I know that people do bad things. They do them for as many different reasons as the complexity of the human mind can explain. But, unless their minds are malfunctioning with some sort of psychosis that hampers logical thought, they have, as the basis for their actions, a form of happiness that they perceive as good for them.

Many years ago, early in my business career, I learned of two very different management styles. Some managers espoused the theory that no one likes or wants to work, so everyone must be pushed or shoved in whatever manner necessary to obtain a day's production out of them. We called those the X-type managers. Then there were managers who felt that people basically wanted to work and took pride in accomplishing a good day's work and the resulting production. We called these Y-type managers.

I apply the Y-type manager approach to life and teaching, meaning I feel that all people, whether young or old, embrace knowledge. Have you ever seen anyone more eager to learn than five- or six-year-old children just beginning their life of formal education? Wouldn't it be fantastic if we could find ways to perpetuate their enthusiasm for learning throughout their lives? Do they actually lose that enthusiasm? Unfortunately, many do, but many just change the way they react to learning. Even the so-called incorrigible kid who always gets into fights and verbally bullies everyone near him enjoys learning new things. According to Dr. Phil McGraw, you just need to find their currency.

I believe the X-type managers have returned and are alive and well in our classrooms. This time they have fueled this approach with their fear of terrorism. If you think that's a big leap, think about how you continuously shrink away from the bully until one day you've had enough. Even though you know he or she could wipe the floor with you, you eventually fight back. Unfortunately, in your case you take out the frustration and fear on the weaker people, your students. Instead of working on understanding the source of your fear, you "bull up," as my mom used to say, and become stricter with your rules, and tougher on your tests, and demand silence in your classrooms. If, when you search into the deepest regions of your soul, you find that the frightening experience of 9/11 has seated itself, there you will also find something far more shocking.

You originally made the career choice to become an educator because you like school and learning. When you began to teach you discovered that there was a lot you had to learn, and so learn it you did. Whether you have been teaching for many years or have just begun, you have this inner desire to learn and understand. However, what you have learned about terrorism so far makes no sense. Therefore, there is no understanding. The news media focuses on current events, and the resultant information they feed us leaves us thinking that the Middle Eastern world hates Americans because they see us as imperialists consumed by worldly things, and because we want to colonize or overcome their world to take their oil and subjugate them. You wonder how those people can feel this way, since you believe we are a peace-loving nation. Harboring those thoughts, along with a lack of knowledge of the Middle Eastern people and culture, deepens your fear of unjustified terrorism.

The Real Reason for Terrorism

Looking at current events will not provide the answer about the mysterious hatred that has caused terrorist attacks on our country and many others. America did not do anything to instill such hatred. America didn't even exist when Muhammad ibn Abdul Wahhab began preaching his version of Sunni Islam, and the resulting violence was never a reaction to imperialists' intrusion into their world. There are no events in recent history that would cause or fuel such a burning hatred.

If you listen to news accounts, and read what you can find on the relationships between our country and those of the Middle East, you may actually find evidence of the hatred of Jews existing in the Arab world. That, combined with our national support of Israeli interests, may be enough to convince yourself of a reason.

However, the history of the American presence in the oil fields of countries like Saudi Arabia reflects our desire for interdependence, not imperialism. We did not use our military might to intimidate the Saudis into accepting our presence there. Our oil companies actually formed a corporation called Aramco and gradually increased Saudi ownership in this until it became 100 hundred percent owned by the Saudi government. We have military bases in Saudi Arabia at the request of the Saudis. Ambassador Dore Gold, president of the Jerusalem Center for Public Affairs and the eleventh Permanent Representative of Israel to the United Nations (1997–1999), and previously foreign policy adviser to the former prime minister of Israel, Benjamin Netanyahu, says in his book *Hatred's Kingdom*: "There was no arrogance of American power, as detractors of the United States try to assert. The blame for the hatred behind September 11 is not at America's doorstep. Rather, as has been seen, Saudi Arabia's own internal development accounts for how such hatred was spawned." Perhaps what reaches our deepest fears is the fact that the Wahhab interpretation of the Islamic beliefs added *jihad*, which literally means "struggle" and is misinterpreted by some to mean "holy war," as the sixth pillar of the Islamic faith.

The Muslim world has been plagued with wars for over a thousand years and found its fervor for intolerance and jihad rekindled by Wahhabism in the eighteenth century. According to Dore Gold's *Hatred's Kingdom*, such organizations and personages as Hamas, the Taliban, and Osama bin Laden came from this radicalism taught in some of Saudi Arabia's schools and mosques.

Understand that this Wahhab interpretation is considered a radical and violent departure from mainstream Islamic faith. The other five pillars of this faith are affirming God and His messengers (declaration of faith), prayer, charity, the Ramadan fast, and the pilgrimage to Mecca. These certainly are honorable, religious, faith-filled, peaceful beliefs.

What Can You Do about This Fear?

Use education to tap into the Muslim belief in those five pillars of faith. The international community must continue setting minimal standards for human behavior, placing the highest value on the sacredness of human life and applying these standards not only to the Western world, but also to the Middle East. Tolerance of inhumane behavior is simply unacceptable, and the vast majority of the Christian, Jewish, and Muslim world believe this. You, then, as an educator, must build support for this international effort to reduce terrorism and your fear of it. You have an excellent opportunity to do this with the lockdown drills.

When explaining to your students what to do in a lockdown drill to keep them as safe as possible in the event of a terrorist or criminal attack, you also should explain the source of the hatred causing this element of society to exist in the world. Learn as much as you can about the root cause and what our country and much of the international community is doing to overcome terrorism.

Just as some of the schools and mosques of Saudi Arabia and other Middle Eastern countries inculcate belief in terrorism to gain the world for Islam, you can educate belief in human rights to gain the world for freedom. I hope I have given you enough information here to reduce your fears and to instill a desire to learn more on this subject.

THE FEAR I am overwhelmed by the daily onslaught of news about terrorist and criminal activity in the world. Every time I read about a senseless shooting or murder, and every time I see rude and inhumane actions going on between my students, I fear the "dark side" is winning. I have students who have a value system of "me first," and whatever it takes to achieve that is okay and right. How do I explain that cheating, rudeness, or bullying is wrong when the "street" and media fill their minds with this to the point of perceived normalcy?

THE SOLUTION No one said life would be easy, especially for a teacher. You must remind yourself daily that you have an opportunity to change the world, if only one person at a time. You have a greater opportunity to do this than does anyone else in any other occupation. The greatest motivational speakers' opportunity pales in comparison with yours. I have commented before about the captive audience you have. Continue even if they feel it is boring sameness, and focus on enthusiastically doing the right thing and teaching about the sources of terrorism and hate. They will notice, and many will carry your model forward into their adult lives, influencing their worlds. Remember the ripples of the pebble thrown into the pond.

LET'S SUMMARIZE . . .

❶ Begin filtering the information you receive about "bad" news through your rose-colored glasses of hope.

❷ Accept the theory that the human mind at all ages actually seeks knowledge.

❸ Find and understand the basis for the terrorism that exists in today's world. Understanding reduces fear.

❹ Take the opportunities presented to you by such things as lockdown drills to teach about the sources of terrorism to your students, thereby reducing both your fear and theirs.

CHAPTER 26

What Do I Do When the Government Interferes?

Feel free to interpret "affairs" any way you want, including "a matter occasioning public anxiety, controversy, or scandal" (sometimes spelled "affaire" in this usage) as defined in *Webster's 11th Collegiate Dictionary*. When looking at government interferences let's keep in mind that our public school system is in fact a government monopoly. Therefore, comparing it to other such monopolies makes perfect sense.

Perhaps many of you remember when Ma Bell (Bell Telephone) provided our phone service. You should also remember that all telephones were black, you could only lease them, all calls were expensive, and it was actually illegal to connect an answering machine because that was a foreign device. However, when the government broke Ma Bell into several companies, the costs went down and you suddenly had a choice of style and color for your phone. Eventually, this led to cell phones and more.

During my business career I had several occasions to travel on government-run airlines and found the service was horrendous; the planes were filthy; the flight attendants were surly; and lateness was the norm. How about the Trabant or the Yugo? These were cars made by the governments of East Germany and Yugoslavia.

They nearly fell apart before purchasers got them home, and the unhappy buyer could not find service or parts anywhere. Should I mention the United States Postal Service? Okay, since I have, do you know why Federal Express and United Parcel Service and a multitude of local express delivery services came into existence? Okay, I'll tell you. Because the U.S. Postal Service was so slow and unreliable that businessmen had to find a better way to move their commerce.

Yet, we continue perpetuating an education system that forces parents to send their children to certain schools (although charter schools have begun to help some). Many kids who can't read at basic levels still graduate from our public high schools. Based on the most recent Organisation of Economic Cooperation and Development (OECD) Programme for International Student Assessment (PISA) test, given to fifteen-year-olds in forty countries, our students came in below average, ranking number twenty-nine in science and number thirty-five in math, behind many much poorer countries. The Associated Press reported that on the 2003 Trends in International Math and Science Test Series (TIMSS), American high school twelfth-graders scored near the bottom of all nations, outperforming only Cyprus and South Africa. So, there you have it: another government-run monopoly, our public school system, has failed us.

Recently John Stossel did a piece on the ABC News show *20/20*. He interviewed a family from South Carolina who had a son in his senior year in a public high school. The son couldn't read at a basic level. Stossel sent him to Sylvan Learning Centers. Within seventy-two hours the student's reading improved by two grade levels, he had begun reading magazines that had regularly come to his home, and started using flash cards to teach himself new words. Stossel commented how sad he thought it was that a public school system couldn't teach the young man how to read after twelve years at a cost of more than $100,000 in tax-payer money, while Sylvan did it in such a short time and for only $3,000. Okay, Sylvan tutored him one-on-one and surely that's an advantage, but three days versus twelve years? Inexcusable.

So Where Does This Leave Us?

It leaves us in quite a quandary. Perhaps this issue engenders more anxiety than fear, but I'm not sure where one stops and the other starts. We have a monster and, at least for the foreseeable future, must live with it.

You know that this failing government monopoly (which is failing our kids) requires standardized testing of the students, and in some states requires testing for you, too. Testing to find out what someone knows or has learned certainly isn't a new or unusual concept. The fact that this device is used isn't the issue. The issue is whether testing accomplishes its task of helping to find ways to make sure every child gets a good education in order to have a shot at the opportunities this country has to offer. If it does, then I think you will agree it's a good thing, well worth the time that you and your students are taken away from your class-room. On the other hand, since the statistics imply that testing is not achieving that objective, why bother? Yet, bother you do, because you have no choice.

The following is a list of a few abbreviations and acronyms symbolizing tests required for high school graduation, college entrance tests, and other miscellaneous tests: AHSGE, HSGQE, AIMS, CHSEE, FCAT, GHSGT, ISAT, GQE, GEE, HSA, MCAS, SATP, HSPE, HSPA, NMHSCE, OGT, EOI, HSAP, TAKS, SOL, WASL, HLM, SAT, ACT, AP tests, CST, CAT, CTBS, CELDT, and MAP. The list goes on and on.

Even though this list represents tests given by the different states, they all resulted from the well-intentioned No Child Left Behind law. And, since federal funding for schools depends to some extent on the results of these tests, the states have essentially "dumbed them down" from time to time to keep the success rates high.

Why Are You Stuck in This Paradigm of Failure?

Some years ago the Clinton administration attempted to create government-run universal health care so everyone would have access to free health care. It failed for various reasons. I wonder whether, if it had succeeded, we would now be facing health care provided to us with the inefficiency of the U.S. Postal Service, or like the high-expense-for-little-option monopolistic telephone system.

In his book *Discovering the Future: The Business of Paradigms,* Joel Arthur Barker tells an interesting story. He calls it "The Final Story: The Pig and the Sow." In essence it's a story about a man who owns a cabin in a mountainous region. He likes to go to his cabin on weekends and especially enjoys driving his Porsche on the steep, narrow road with its sharp, blind curves. On one trip, just as he approached one such blind curve, he heard the screeching tires of a car coming his way. He slowed to nearly a stop when the other car came around the curve while weaving in and out of its lane, nearly out of control. He held his breath in fear that he would be hit. As the car passed him in a near miss, its female driver yelled out the window at him the word "pig." Insulted by that, he yelled back, "sow." He then calmed himself before starting back toward the blind curve, feeling a bit smug at having gotten in such an appropriate retort for her blatant disregard for his safety. He felt so good about himself that he mashed down on the accelerator and roared into the curve, hitting a large pig standing in the center of the road.

Does this mean that you shouldn't feel such anxiety over having to take time out of your teaching day for these state-required tests, which should serve to reduce or eliminate the fear you have of not adequately teaching your students? What would happen if, instead of fretting over the time "lost" with these tests, you spent that time looking for ways to make better use of the results of the tests, or ways to demonstrate the lack of need for those tests? Taking this road could reap tremendous rewards, but offering this sort of change could present another risk to you. The administration may not accept your suggestions, which might place your career working in that school in jeopardy.

Attempting change always comes with risk in our society, and knowing that would increase your level of anxiety. So, should you continue with the status quo level of fear that isn't going away, or go for a new one that offers the potential of great satisfaction? I suggest going for the change, because the evidence of the failure of the status quo demands it. Establish your approach by taking the following steps:

1. Gain statistical support from your state department of education and the U.S. Department of Education showing the ineffectiveness of the status quo.
2. Talk to parents of your students. Also talk to area business-people; any of the human resource staff of any company can tell you about the frustrations they experience in finding qualified people.
3. If you find a sense of need for change, and I am certain you will, take notes on the ideas from these various sources.
4. Summarize these notes into an organized document, and present all your ideas to your administration, academic

committee, dean of students, or anyone else who may have some ability to effect a change. Expect resistance as a natural human response.

5. Continue listening to your sources, as mentioned in step number two. In the world of business we call these people our customers and suppliers, and we can't survive without them.

6. Go back to your administration to follow up and to provide new ideas.

7. You may need to continue listening, talking, and presenting ideas for quite some time. Change never comes easily, especially when dealing with a monopoly.

Small parts of your ideas may begin to become the standard or an evolving paradigm that will eventually become the new paradigm. As the successes of the new paradigm become noticed, the resistance diminishes and the new paradigm becomes the old paradigm in need of more study.

Does taking all these steps seem like a lot of extra work when you already have a lot on your plate? In reality, talking to parents, students, and businesspeople should be part of your normal routine anyway, so you simply add a couple of questions. If you consider the alternative, which is that anxiety and fear will not go away unless changes are made, the work involved achieving the change becomes well worth it.

In summary, I have taken you from having a state of fear and anxiety related to government-mandated testing to the steps you can take to remove both.

THE FEAR I find I must teach to the state graduation tests because my students must pass these to graduate. I have some students who lack the ability to pass those tests no matter how hard they try, or how well I teach.

THE SOLUTION Most counties in most states offer vocational schools free for students up to age twenty-one. Talk to your administrator about these as alternatives for those students. We need people who have the skills of artisans, auto mechanics, chefs, hairdressers, and so on.

LET'S SUMMARIZE . . .

❶ The issue of standardized testing goes deeper than the time it takes to administer the tests and the fact that they take the students from the classrooms. It involves the functioning of our whole education system.

❷ Think about the success or failure of our current public school system, and what can be done to change it for the better.

❸ Review the actual tests for graduation. How do the questions asked compare to what you teach?

❹ Review the seven steps you can take to change the system.

Additional Resources

Teacher Organizations

American Federation of Teachers

The AFT is a teacher's union associated with the AFL-CIO. Among other resources, it provides educators with support and legal aid. It also lobbies congressional leaders concerning educational issues. *www.aft.org*

American Library Association

The ALA is the oldest and largest library association in the world. Members include librarians from the public sector, universities, and schools across the nation and the world. *www.ala.org*

Association for Supervision and Curriculum Development

According to their website, ASCD represents "all aspects of effective teaching and learning." While focused more upon administrators and professional development, there is much pertinent information here. *www.ascd.org*

Council for Exceptional Children

This organization is dedicated to improving the education provided to gifted students and those with disabilities and varying exceptionalities. *www.cec.sped.org/ab/*

International Reading Association
The International Reading Association is dedicated to promoting literacy for all students and individuals. *www.reading.org*

National Council for Teachers of English
This organization helps bring together English and language arts teachers and provides them with information, resources, and more. *www.ncte.org/homepage*

National Council for Teachers of Mathematics
This council provides educators with excellent information and resources pertinent to the world of math. *www.nctm.org*

National Council for the Social Studies
Find out the latest news for social studies teachers, including standards and more. *www.ncss.org*

National Education Association
The NEA is a teacher's union that traces its roots back to 1857. The group does many things including lobbying congressional leaders concerning educational issues and providing legal support for educators. *www.nea.org*

National Science Teachers Association
This organization allows science teachers to investigate the latest educational and scientific developments. *www.nsta.org*

United States Distance Learning Association
This association provides information, advocacy, and opportunities for distance learning educators. *www.usdla.org*

Online Resources

About.com Elementary School Educators

An About.com site providing excellent lesson plans, resources, and information for elementary school (K–6) educators. *http://k-6educators.about.com*

About.com Secondary School Educators

This site provides lesson plans, resources, information on educational issues, advice, chats, and discussions for secondary school (6–12) educators. *http://7-12educators.about.com*

About.com Private Schools

This site focuses on issues specific to private schools. It is an excellent resource if you plan on teaching in this environment and includes lesson plans, resources, and information. *http://privateschools.about.com*

B. F. Skinner Foundation

Learn more about operant conditioning and positive/negative reinforcement at this interesting website. *www.bfskinner.org/index.asp*

Education Week

Read the latest daily and weekly news from Education Week. You can sign up for free access. *www.edweek.org*

Education World

Another great site for teachers. Find lesson plans, information on professional development, educational news, and an area devoted specifically to administration. *www.education-world.com*

ERIC Clearinghouse on Disabilities and Gifted Education

The Educational Resources Information Center (ERIC) provides a wealth of information for teaching gifted students and those with disabilities. *http://ericec.org*

Florida Virtual School

Here is the website for the Florida Virtual School, the first state-funded virtual school. *www.flvs.net*

Free Things for Educators

Excellent site providing information for free online and offline resources available to all levels of educators. *www.freethings4educators.com*

IDEA Practices

This excellent site will help you understand the ins and outs of Individuals with Disabilities Education Act (IDEA) and how it affects you. *www.ideapractices.org/index.php*

National Center for Education Statistics

Learn more about the latest statistics collected about education across the United States. *http://nces.ed.gov/index.html*

U.S. Department of Education

Learn about the latest policies and initiatives affecting the nation's classrooms. *www.ed.gov/index.jsp*

Departments of Education Websites by State

Alabama *www.alsde.edu/html/home.asp*

Alaska *www.educ.state.ak.us*

Arizona *www.ade.state.az.us*

Arkansas *http://arkedu.state.ar.us*

California *http://goldmine.cde.ca.gov*

Colorado *www.cde.state.co.us*

Connecticut *www.state.ct.us/sde*

Delaware *www.doe.state.de.us*

District of Columbia *www.k12.dc.us/dcps/home.html*

Florida *www.fldoe.org*

Georgia *www.doe.k12.ga.us*

Hawaii *http://doe.k12.hi.us*

Idaho *www.sde.state.id.us/Dept*

Illinois *www.isbe.state.il.us*

Indiana *http://ideanet.doe.state.in.us*

Iowa *www.state.ia.us/educate/index.html*

Kansas *www.ksbe.state.ks.us/Welcome.html*

Kentucky *www.kde.state.ky.us*

Louisiana *www.doe.state.la.us/lde/index.html*

Maine *www.state.me.us/education/homepage.htm*

Maryland *www.msde.state.md.us*

Massachusetts *www.doe.mass.edu*

Michigan *www.michigan.gov/mde*

Minnesota *http://education.state.mn.us/stellent/groups/public/documents/ translatedcontent/pub_mde_home.jsp*

Mississippi *www.mde.k12.ms.us*

Missouri *http://services.dese.state.mo.us/index.html*

Montana *www.opi.state.mt.us/index.html*

Nebraska *www.nde.state.ne.us*

Nevada *www.nde.state.nv.us*

New Hampshire *www.ed.state.nh.us*

New Jersey *www.state.nj.us/education*

New Mexico *www.sde.state.nm.us/index.html*

New York *www.nysed.gov*

North Carolina *www.dpi.state.nc.us*

North Dakota *www.dpi.state.nd.us/index.shtm*

Ohio *www.ode.state.oh.us*

Oklahoma *www.sde.state.ok.us/home/defaultie.html*

Pennsylvania *www.pde.state.pa.us/pde_internet/site/default.asp*

Rhode Island *www.ridoe.net*

South Carolina *www.sde.state.sc.us*

South Dakota *www.state.sd.us/deca*

Tennessee *www.state.tn.us/education*

Texas *www.tea.state.tx.us*

Utah *www.usoe.k12.ut.us*

Vermont *www.state.vt.us/educ*

Virginia *www.pen.k12.va.us*

Washington *www.sbe.wa.gov*

West Virginia *http://wvde.state.wv.us*

Wisconsin *www.dpi.state.wi.us*

Wyoming *www.k12.wy.us/index.htm*

APPENDIX B

Bibliography and Sources Cited

Bibliography

ABC News. Oct. 21, 2005. Do "helicopter moms" do more harm than good? *http://abcnews.go.com/print?id=1237868.*

Administration for Children & Families. 2005. Child maltreatment. Victimization rates by age group, 2005. Chaps. 3 and 5. *www.acf.hhs.gov/programs/cb/pubs/cm05/figure3_3.htm.*

Anderson Orr, Anissa, and Karen Krakower. 2006. Understanding sudden death in teen athletes. *Health Leader.* The University of Texas Health Science Center at Houston. *www.healthleader.uthouston.edu/archive/Children_Teens/2004/sudden-death-0923.html.*

Associated Press. March 29, 2006. Report: More than a quarter of U.S. schools fail to meet law's requirements. FoxNews.com.

Association of American Educators. AAE teacher liability insurance. *www.aaeteachers.org/insurance.shtml.*

Atkinson, Philip. July 25, 2007. Political correctness. *www.ourcivilisation.com/pc.htm.*

Beavers, Sean. 2007. Online rubric generators: a grading time-saver! *SOITA Updater* XXVIII, no. 1.

Bill & Melinda Gates Foundation. Annual Report 2003: Education. *www.gatesfoundation.org/nr/public/media/annualreports/annualreport03/HTML/education.html.*

Bleifuss, Joel. February 21, 2007. A politically correct lexicon. *www.inthesetimes.com?article/3027/a_politically_correct_lexicon.*

Bonfadini, John E. 1993. Discipline: education's number one problem. Virginia Council on Technology Teacher Education. Monograph 2. *www.teched.vy.edu/VCTTE/VCTTEMonographs/VCTTEMono2(Discipline).html.*

Cantor, Andrea. 2005. Test protocols and parents rights—to copies? *Communiqué.* Vol. 34, 1.

Carroll, Felix. January 27, 2005. No escape from "helicopter parents." *Seattle Post-Intelligencer.* *http://seattlepi.nwsource.com/lifestyle/209473_copterparents.html.*

Center for Effective Collaboration and Practice. *http://cecp.air.org/interact/authoronline/february99/3.htm.*

Center for Justice and Democracy. April 20, 2001. Federal immunity for corporal punishment—why it's a bad idea. *www.nospank.net/federal.htm.*

Center for Justice and Democracy. Mythbuster! Teacher immunity and disciplinary abuse. *www.centerjd.org/private/mythbuster/MB_school_teacher_immunity/htm.*

Coping with the sudden death of a pupil. October 6, 2007. *www.teachernet.gov.uk/wholeschool/healthandsafety/pupilfatality.*

Crain, William. 2003. *Reclaiming Childhood: Letting Children Be Children in Our Achievement-Oriented Society.* New York: Henry Holt.

Education Commission of the States. 2007. Exit exams: state requires passage of exit exam for high school graduation. *http://mb2.ecs.org/reports/Report.aspx?id=1359.*

Elliott, Scott. 2007. Dayton board lays off 208 teachers. *Dayton Daily News.* June 20, 2007.

ERIC Clearinghouse on Counseling and Personnel Services. October 6, 2007. Suicide and sudden loss: crisis management in the schools. An ERIC/CAPS Digest. *www.ericdigests.org/pre-9214/loss.htm.*

Esquith, Rafe. 2007. *Teach Like Your Hair's On Fire.* New York: Viking.

Federal Government Spending Report. Picture Summary of 5 Core Threats.

Giesen, Carol A. B. 1995. *Coal Miners' Wives.* Lexington, KY: University Press of Kentucky.

Glassner, Barry. 1999. *The Culture of Fear.* New York: Basic Books.

Goldring, Ellen B. March 1990. Principals' relationships with parents: The homogeneity versus the social class of the parent clientele. *The Urban Review.* Vol. 22, 1.

Hodges, Michael. *Dangerous Erosion of Education Quality & Productivity.* Grandfather Economic Report. *http://mwhodges.home.att.net.*

Lewin, Tamar. 2005. Nationwide survey includes data on teenage sex habits. *New York Times.* September 16.

Maxym, Carol, and Leslie B. York. 2000. *Teens in Turmoil.* New York: Viking.

Muller, Wayne. 2002. *Legacy of the Heart.* New York: Fireside.

The National View. September 10, 2007. Leaving no child behind. *www.washingtonpost.com/wp-dyn/content/article/2007/09/09/ AR2007090901247.html.*

Newberger, Julee. April 7, 2001. Corporal punishment in schools. *Connect for Kids. www.connectforkids.org/node/265.*

O'Reilly, Bill. 2006. *Culture Warrior.* New York: Broadway Books.

Peale, Norman Vincent. 1961. *The Tough Minded Optimist.* New York: Fawcett Crest.

Ponder, Phil. 2007. Terror thumbs a ride on school buses. *Cincinnati Enquirer.* April 3.

Rosemond, John. 2007. Calling a thorn a rose is prickly advice. *Dayton Daily News.* August 6.

Sarafino, Edward P. 1986. *The Fears of Childhood.* New York: Human Sciences Press.

Serra, Richard. 2007. Parental neglect causes behavior problems in children. *www.helium.com/tm/196027/parents-short-takes-raise.*

Sexual Harassment Support. Hostile environment harassment defined. *www.sexualharassmentsupport.org/index.html.*

Shellenbarger, Sue. May 9, 2007. Helicopter parents now hover at the office. The Wall Street Journal Online.

———. July 29, 2005. Colleges ward off overinvolved parents. Career Journal.com. The Wall Street Journal Online.

Sizer, Theodore R., and Nancy Faust Sizer. 1999. *The Students Are Watching.* Boston: Beacon Press.

Teenage Homosexuality. 2007. *www.planetpapers.com/Assets/1506.php.*

Thattai, Deeptha. Sept. 15, 2007. A history of public education in the United States. *www.servintfree.net/~aidmn-ejournal/publications/2001-11.*

Sources Cited

Barker, Joel Arthur. 1993. *Discovering the Future: The Business of Paradigms.* New York: Harper Business.

Carnegie, Dale. 2005. *Public Speaking for Success.* Rev. and updated by Arthur R. Pell. New York: Penguin.

Center for Justice and Democracy. Federal immunity for corporal punishment—why it's a bad idea. *www.nospank.net/federal.htm.*

Child Welfare Information Gateway. *http://basis.caliber.com/cwig/ws/library/docs/gateway/Record.*

Child Welfare League of America. National data analysis system. *http://ndas.cwla.org/data_stats/access/predefined/Report.*

Closson, Don. 1992. Probe Ministries politically correct education. Probe Ministries International. *www.leaderu.com/orgs/probe/docs/pc-educ.html.*

deKoster, Katie, ed. 1994. *Child Abuse: Opposing Viewpoints.* San Diego, CA: Greenhaven Press.

Franks, Tommy. August 2004. *American Soldier.* New York: Harper Collins.

Gold, Dore. 2003. *Hatred's Kingdom.* Washington, DC: Regnery Publishing, Inc.

Grandfather Economic Report Series. *http://mwhodges.home.att.net/education.htm.*

Grandfather Economic Report Series. Dangerous erosion of education quality & productivity. *http://mhodges.home.att.net/education.htm.*

Harris, Louis. 1969. The Life poll. *Life.*

Hooper, Bayard. 1969. The task is to learn what learning is for. *Life.*

Jeffers, Susan. 2007. *Feel the Fear—and Do It Anyway.* New York: Ballantine Books.

Johnson, Helen and Christine Schelhas-Miller. 2000. *Don't Tell Me What to Do, Just Send Money.* New York: St. Martin's Press.

Kohl, Herbert. 1994. *I Won't Learn from You.* New York: New Press.

Kozol, Jonathan. 1991. *Savage Inequalities.* New York: Crown Publishing Group.

Krzyzewski, Mike. 2000. *Leading with the Heart.* New York: Warner Books.

Lawlis, Frank. 2004. *The ADD Answer.* New York: Viking.

National Center for Education Statistics. 2006. Indicators of school crime and safety: 2006. *http://nces.ed.gov/programs/crimeondicators/crimeindicators2007/ind_19.asp.*

Nelson, Ted. 1974. *Computer Lib/Dream Machines, Revised Edition.* Redmond, Washington: Microsoft Press.

New Hampshire Bureau of Emergency Medical Services and EMS for Children Project at Dartmouth Medical School. November 2003. Public access defibrillation in New Hampshire schools. Concord, New Hampshire.

Pittman, Frank. 1989. *Private Lies: Infidelity and the Betrayal of Intimacy.* New York: Norton.

Sexual Harassment Support. Sexual harassment in education. *www.sexualharassmentsupport.org/SHEd.html.*

Stossel, John. 2004. *Give Me A Break.* New York: HarperCollins.

———. 2006. *Myths, Lies, and Downright Stupidity.* New York: Hyperion.

U.S. Department of Labor Bureau of Labor Statistics. 2003. Tomorrow's jobs. *www.bls.gov/oco/oco2003.htm.*

Index